Best of All Is Jesus

Best of All Is Jesus

Alger Fitch

COLLEGE PRESS PUBLISHING COMPANY
Joplin, Missouri 64802

Copyright © 1991
College Press Publishing Company

Printed and Bound in the
United States of America
All Rights Reserved

Library of Congress Catalog Card Number: 90-55860
International Standard Book Number: 0-89900-389-3

TABLE OF CONTENTS

Preface.....7

Introduction.....11
Hebrews as Sermon, Sermon Standard and Sermon-starter

PART ONE
Jesus, The Bearer Of God's Clearest Message

CHAPTER ONE.....21
The New Is Better

CHAPTER TWO.....31
Be an Angel

CHAPTER THREE.....41
So Great a Salvation

CHAPTER FOUR.....53
A Long Way to Paradise

PART TWO
Jesus, The Provider Of God's Greatest Deliverance

CHAPTER FIVE.....63
Half Way to Glory

CHAPTER SIX.....73
The Sabbath That Remains

CHAPTER SEVEN.....85
Piercing Sword or Protective Shield

PART THREE
Jesus, The Offerer of God's Holiest Intercession

CHAPTER EIGHT.....97
A Priest That Is Different

CHAPTER NINE.....107
You Ought To Be Teachers

CHAPTER TEN.....117
Red Flares and Vanishing Clouds

CHAPTER ELEVEN.....127
Meet Your King

PART FOUR
Jesus, The Maker of God's Finest Covenant

CHAPTER TWELVE.....141
There Is a Difference

CHAPTER THIRTEEN.....151
Who Moved the Furniture?

CHAPTER FOURTEEN.....161
Where There's a Will, There's a Way

CHAPTER FIFTEEN.....171
Waiting for the Second Coming

CHAPTER SIXTEEN.....181
When God Forgets

CHAPTER SEVENTEEN.....189
We Shrink Not Back

PART FIVE
Jesus, The Appealer To Man's Purest Motives

CHAPTER EIGHTEEN.....203
Audio-visual Faith

CHAPTER NINETEEN.....215
Amen! Ouch!

CHAPTER TWENTY.....225
Choosing Mountains

CHAPTER TWENTY ONE.....235
Jesus Never Fails

CHAPTER TWENTY TWO.....247
Eyes on the Future

Conclusion.....257
Choose the Best

Appendix.....259
One Preacher's Analysis of Another Preacher's Sermon: Hebrews in Outline

PREFACE

Many religions compete for the total allegiance of each person on earth. Leaders of minor cults and significant figures in major world-wide faiths both ask for and receive the trust of large numbers of people. Since one's thoughts and acts inevitably are shaped by what that person considers the highest good, the choice of one's spiritual leader is the most consequential of all of life's options.

If God is like Jesus of Nazareth, how hopeful man's future can be. The poor and the weak found encouragement in his words. The sick by his touch were restored to wholeness. The wayward, through his grace, were helped to believe they could be transformed into God's children. Jesus had power, but only used that omnipotence to bless and not to blight. Jesus was unquestionably holy, but never aloof from sinners who needed to hear his inclusive call to forgiveness and new birth.

BEST OF ALL IS JESUS

The writer of Hebrews grew up under the divinely revealed religion of Judaism. In grateful appreciation for his background, he rejoiced in the Messianic hope that the law and the prophets had kindled. He discovered in Jesus of Nazareth what every other disciple of Christ had found. God had not sent His Messiah for but one people of earth. Rather, God had "so loved the world that he gave his only begotten son" (John 3:16)[1] for humans "of every tribe, and tongue, and people and nation" (Revelation 5:9). The conclusion of every person who has opted for Christianity is that as good as any religion may claim to be, the religion of Christ proves to be "better." "Better" is the word found again and again in the epistle of Hebrews. Without challenging the Jew's claim that the world's Creator and Sustainer had delivered them from Egyptian bondage and made them into a special people, the church claims that the Saviour who was born to the Jewess Mary had instituted the "better" way available now to every man and woman on earth.

To read the epistle to the Hebrews is to hear the gentle persuasion that "best of all is Jesus." Paul agrees that "in the name of Jesus every knee should bow . . . and that every tongue should confess that Jesus Christ is Lord, to the glory of God the Father" (Phil. 2:10-11). Peter gives his nod of agreement when he says, "God hath made him both Lord and Christ, this Jesus whom ye crucified" (Acts 2:36). John at the end of the apostolic age wrote, "Worthy is the Lamb that hath been slain to receive the power, and riches, and wisdom, and might, and honor, and glory, and blessing" (Rev. 5:12).

The carpenter that was born in Bethlehem, ministered in Galilee and died and rose again in Jerusalem, is a stark contrast to most religious figures. Where there are points of comparison with other gentle and wise teachers, the fitting word that keeps coming to describe Jesus is the comparative "better."

Let each religion examine the lives and teachings of the leaders that brought forth the given world faiths. Let each individual use the mind God gave to all of his human creatures. Let him use the will that Deity has placed within him. Let him opt for the best. No other decision is worthy of one created in the image of God. In any careful and thorough examination, I anticipate you will be compelled to conclude with the author of Hebrews that *Best of All Is Jesus*.

Endnotes

1. Scripture quotations unless otherwise noted are from the American Standard Version (Thomas Nelson & Sons: New York, 1901).

INTRODUCTION

Hebrews as Sermon, Sermon-standard and Sermon-starter

Hebrews is a sermon. Hebrews is also a standard by which to measure sermons. It is my conviction that Hebrews can be a starter for many a helpful sermon.

HEBREWS AS A SERMON OF SERMONS

There are sermons in the Bible easily recognizable as such. World renowned is Jesus' Sermon on the Mount (Matt. 5-7). The book of Acts preserves sermons from the lips of Peter (2,3,10), Stephen (7), Philip (8), and Paul (13,17,20). Men such as C.H. Dodd and Willie Marxsen are quick to term the Gospel of Mark as *predict* or preaching. Others speak of I Peter as a baptismal homily or of I John as more a sermon than an epistle. At least I John begins and ends less like a letter and more like a sermon with its opening and closing sentences.

The author of Hebrews describes his own writing by labeling it a "word of exhortation." As he draws the work to a close, he pens these words just prior to the salutation and benediction: "But I exhort you brethren, bear with the word of exhortation: for I have written unto you in few words" (Heb. 13:22). Compare this teminology to Acts 13:15, which precedes Paul's sermon at Antioch of Pisidia: "And after the reading of the law and the prophets the rulers of the synagogue sent unto them (Paul and Barnabas) saying, Brethren, if ye have any word of exhortation for the people, say on." Apparently "word of exhortation" was the common phrase for instruction from the Scripture.

At least Hebrews begins like a sermon, progresses like a sermon and ends like a sermon. We can conclude that it was penned by a preacher, whether written by Paul, Apollos or some other person. It begins with an opening sentence about God as a communicator: "God, having of old time spoken unto the fathers in the prophets by divers portions and in divers manners, hath at the end of these days spoken unto us in his Son" (1:1-2). It has for its proposition that Jesus is "better" in every way than all that preceded in Old Testament times. That word "better" is used thirteen times. Hebrews moves from doctrine to appeal and life application throughout.[1] All of the epistle is directed to the practical needs of a particular people in approximately 68 A.D.

Oversimplified, the structure of the sermon is something like this. Christ is a better messenger than prophets and angels (Chapters 1-2). He is a better deliverer than Moses and Joshua (Chapters 3-4). He is a better mediator than Aaronic priests and Melchizedek

INTRODUCTION

(Chapter 5-7). His covenant with the church is better than that with Israel (Chapters 8-10). His plea is for Christians to keep their faith (11), hope (12) and love (13).[2]

HEBREWS AS A STANDARD FOR SERMONS

No one can read the sermon, which is Hebrews, without sensing that this preacher loves his Lord, loves his Bible, loves his people and loves to preach. If some one in future years should run across a message you had delivered, would his reading of that lesson convince him that your love was genuine in the same four-square way?

From the opening sentence of Hebrews, it is evident that the author thinks highly of Jesus Christ. He calls him God's

> Son, whom he appointed heir of all things, through whom also he made the worlds; who being the effulgence of his glory, and the very image of his substance, and upholding all things by the word of his power, when he had made purification for sins, sat down on the right hand of the Majesty of high; having become by so much better than the angels (1:1-4).

This sermon exalts Christ. It affirms his pre-existence and heralds his incarnation. It holds high his cross and proclaims his resurrection. No question is left regarding Jesus as the priest *par-excellence*, who is ready to offer "mercy, and . . . grace to help" (4:16), as "he ever liveth to make intercession" (7:25). No doubt is allowed to remain regarding the promised return of the Saviour, for he "shall appear a second time, apart from sin, to them that wait for him unto salvation" (9:28). Origen said only God knows who wrote Hebrews. Yet everyone knows that this author loved and respected the Scriptures of Israel. His first remark was that it was "God" who in "old time" had "spoken unto the fathers in the prophets" (1:1). In quoting a prophet or a psalmist, our author reminds the reader that the Divine voice was behind the human messenger. He would precede the quotation with words like, "even as the Holy Spirit saith" (3:7), or "the Holy Spirit also beareth witness to us; for . . . he hath said" (10:15). The listener sensed that in each quotation he was hearing a "thus saith the Lord." The preacher knew "the word of God" as "living, and active, and sharper than any two-edged sword and piercing even to the dividing of soul and spirit, of both joints and marrow, and quick to discern the thoughts and intents of the heart" (4:12).

Sermons reveal a spokesman's love for Jesus by what he says about him. They overtly or tacitly make plain the speaker's love of Scripture by how those Scriptures are used by him. They also give evidence of the pastor's love for his people. You see it between the lines as well as in the sentences. The choice of topics, the selection of texts and the use of words all uncover the shepherd's concern for his flock. No one can read Hebrews (especially, 2:18; 3:1-6,14; 4:14-16; 5:2-3; 6:12,15; 7:25; 8:12; 10:19,22-25; 12:12 or 13:5) without hearing the beat of a minister's heart. That preacher was no play actor. There is no pretending. There is knowledge about people and their plight. Where they hurt, he hurts. In their dangerous condition, he cares. All sermons can

INTRODUCTION

well be tested by such a norm.
As a preacher, I can tell that this gospel herald loved to preach. The oral reading of Hebrews takes fifty minutes. From point one to final conclusion, we see a pastor encouraging his people. From A to Z, we observe an evangelistic heart calling for decisions. From what we term chapter 1 to the final paragraph of chapter 13, we meet a homiletician structuring his thoughts.

Is it true that Philip the evangelist "opened his mouth, and beginning from . . . Scripture preached . . . Jesus" (Acts 8:35)? So did our author. Did Peter the spokesman for the Twelve reason, "Let all the house of Israel therefore know assuredly, that God hath made him both Lord and Christ, this Jesus" (Acts 2:36)? So did the writer of Hebrews. Did Paul, the master preacher believe sermons were to bring "edification, and exhortation, and consolation" (I Cor. 14:2)? The book of Hebrews passes the test. Do modern professors of homiletics encourage young preacher-boys to speak on only vital themes and ever with clear outlines? Then the first century sample before us makes a supreme example.

HEBREWS AS A STARTER FOR SERMONS

Any sermon worthy of the name must be the sure word of God speaking to the specific needs of men. No book is more filled with solid teaching on topics practical at this hour than is Hebrews. Today people need to see Jesus and the Christian faith tested by comparison with all competitors. In this eclectic day that puts all religions on equal footing, how should we consider Buddha and Mohammed, gurus and seers, with God's only Son? Can Christians be true to Jesus' claims regarding himself as unique and yet avoid the charge of antisemitism? All week your people have been exposed to T.V. evangelists promoting the doctrines of Calvinism, Pentecostalism, eschatological Dispensationalism or some other "ism." They deserve knowing of the option of simple apostolic Christianity. Thus they need sermons that are expository journeys through Bible books like Hebrews, that do not read into the passages new doctrines but discover from the texts what was originally there.

Teaching content, in every sermon of a series, leaves behind a Biblically literate congregation. That congregation will not be led easily into some cult that reduces the Biblical Jesus to the status of a created being like an angel. Such a Scripturally knowledgeable church will be appreciative of knowing why the New Covenant forms are followed in New Testament churches in ways that vary from synagogue and temple practices. It is impossible to imagine a people guided step by step through Hebrews that would not feel Christ's tender forgiveness, know Jesus' full deity and grasp the finality of the revelation that came through him.

A stroll through Hebrews will turn one's eyes from Jerusalem to heaven. It will direct one's path from the Mid-East and its Promised Land to the abiding and heavenly kingdom of God. Those following the full journey will be more faithful in life, more certain in hope and more abounding in love. The mind will better

INTRODUCTION

understand the high place Old Testament Scriptures played in New Testament congregations. The human will shall be more firmly established in its choice to follow Jesus. So onward through the chapters of the special New Testament book of Hebrews. "Bon Voyage" to the exciting truths ahead of you. Sail on to the final destination with enjoyable stops at each port of call.

Endnotes

1. Doctrine (1:1-14; 2:5-3:6; 4:14-5:10; 7:1-10:22; 11:1-12:2; 12:18-29). Exhortation (2:1-4; 3:7-4:13; 5:11-6:20; 10:23-39; 12:3-17; 13:1-25).
2. For my personal extensive analysis of the book see the appendix.

PART ONE
Jesus, the Bearer of God's Clearest Message

CHAPTER ONE

The New Is Better
Hebrews 1:1-3

(The Newness of the Message)

The opening word of Hebrews is "God" (1:1). The last word of the Epistle is "Amen" (13:25). The key to all the words in between is the single word "better."

The author of this sermon is telling some Jewish Christians that, if they should leave Christianity and return to Judaism, they would be deceiving themselves. They could say that they were not leaving Jehovah. They might reason that they would still have the Biblical revelation of the prophets and be a part of a great religion. They needed to know that they were leaving the highest point of God's self-disclosure to something lower. The book of Hebrews shouts loud and clear that Christianity is in every sense "better." Let me repeat that, in this letter's thirteen chapters, thirteen times "better" is the word used to contrast the gospel with the law that preceded it.

THE MESSAGE IS BETTER

The opening verses herald some wonderful things about God. The first in the list is that He communicates with His creatures. "God, having of old time spoken unto the fathers in the prophets by divers portions and in divers manners, hath at the end of these days spoken unto us in his Son" (1:1-2). Isn't our Creator gracious? He does not leave people in ignorance. He speaks to them. He wants them to know His will and His plans on their behalf. So, God in ancient days spoke. But then he was speaking through servants. He was communicating through prophets He would raise up. Today our heavenly Father talks to us through His own Son.

When a prophet received divine revelation, the Holy Spirit came upon him. But in those instances, the Spirit of God came upon that prophet momentarily while the message was being given. In the case of Jesus, the Spirit ever abides in him. Colossians 2:9 speaks of Christ and how "in him dwelleth all the fulness of the Godhead bodily." Thus we can conclude that the Christian message Jesus brought is better than the prophetic message given so long ago. The prophetic message was received in "divers portions and in divers manners" (Heb. 1:1). That is, sometimes revelation came by visions, other times by dreams, and still other times by verbal or direct communication. That Old Testament truth can be called small by contrast to the vast information about God brought through Jesus, His Son.

To use the illustration of Alexander Campbell, we might compare to "starlight" the revelation that came to

THE NEW IS BETTER

patriarchs like Adam, Noah, Abraham and others. The "moonlight" days of Moses and Israel's prophets increased the light in which men might walk after God. But the moonlight and starlight which we had in the Jewish and patriarchal dispensations is not to be compared with the light of God's Sun (God's Son) that now blazes in history since the incarnation. Stars and moon give some light, but nothing compared to the illumination that comes when the sun begins to shine.

When an Old Covenant prophet spoke, he created hope as he predicted the future. All together we find over three hundred predictions in the ancient Scriptures about the coming Messiah. That is wonderful. Yet, how much better is the fulfillment than the bare promise. Here a little and there a little came some promises and some information in olden times. Now that Jesus has come in the flesh, the world can look at him and know what the Father is really like. Of course we appreciate the prophet's message of yesterday. It was God who spoke of old time through such prophets. It is God who speaks today in his Son and that is even better.

THE MEDIATION IS BETTER

The author of Hebrews set out seven things about Jesus in his opening sentence that you could never say about an angel. Let us number these. One, this Son is "heir of all things." Two, "through (him) he made the worlds." Three, he is "the effulgence of his glory." Four, he is "the very image of his substance." Five, he is "upholding all things by the word of his power." Six, he "made purification of sins." And seven, he "sat down on the right hand of the Majesty on high."

We note that you could say hundreds of things about Jesus, but our author selects seven because seven is such an important number in the Scripture. Having listed seven truths about God's Son that could never be attributed to a created being such as an angel, he then begins quoting Old Testament texts. Have you counted them? Will it surprise you to learn that following the seven attributes of Christ will come quotations from seven Old Testament passages? Have you noted that every citation, like every description of Jesus, proves him to be more than an angel? They were "ministering spirits" (Heb. 1:14) as the prophets were ministering servants. Christ was more. His message was fuller. His religion is "better." Jesus was Immanuel, or God in our very midst. What angel, or prophet, could "make purification of sins" (Hebrews 1:3)?

From the fall of Adam, sin had to be reckoned with. Every person born since the first man became a part of fallen humanity. All were sinners and "the wages of sin is death" (Rom. 6:23). That is why priests were raised up. They were to be mediators between sinful people and the holy God of heaven.

How is Jesus a "better" mediator than the priests who preceded him? The Old Testament priests had to first sacrifice for their own sins (Heb. 5:3; 7:27). The Saviour had no sins of his own for which to offer sacrifice. He rather was "holy, guileless, undefiled, separated from sinners, and made higher than the heavens" (Heb. 7:26). He, alone, could look at his neighbors and thrust forth the challenge: "Which of you

convicteth me of sin?" (John 8:46).
The Christian has in Jesus no priest that is a sinner himself. It was the sinless Christ that took upon himself the sins of the world. Go back to Old Testament days. The law taught that where there was sin there would follow the penalty of death. Graciously, God intervened. The law's demand must be kept. Death must follow. But God allowed that an innocent lamb without spot or blemish could die in the sinner's place — the innocent for the guilty. That is, the animal could be the vicarious substitute. The requirement demanded a spotless victim. We have spots. Our lives are marred. As humans we have partaken of the forbidden and left undone the right. Eternal death awaits all mortals unless God's spotless Lamb through a vicarious death covers our sins. Clearly the book of Hebrews affirms that "it is impossible that the blood of bulls and goats should take away sin" (10:4).

What a contrast to Old Testament days we enjoy in New Covenant times. Then there were sinful priests offering animal sacrifices that could not take away even one sin. At best they could but picture the coming day when God would provide the Lamb that could handle the sin problem. The constant offering of sheep on the altar readied the world for the announcement of John the Baptist, "Behold, the Lamb of God, that taketh away the sin of the world" (John 1:29). The prophet's audience understood the matter. They knew man was sinful. They comprehended that God in his goodness had promised to provide the substitutionary sacrifice. They discerned that no animal's life would suffice to remove the penalty. They grasped that God's love, mercy and wisdom could devise the way that humanity's need could be met by deity's self-giving. They would later see that Jesus, God's Son, was that perfect sin-offering. As Immanuel, or God in flesh, he could give himself the ransom for the many.

Hear afresh Paul's words to the Ephesian elders. Listen as if you had never listened to them before! "Take heed unto yourselves, and to all the flock, in which the Holy Spirit hath made you bishops, to feed the church of the Lord which he purchased with his own blood" (Acts 20:28). You need to know that some ancient manuscripts, including the two oldest ones, read "the church of *God* which *he* purchased with *his* own blood." The invisible God is said to have blood. God, who is spirit (John 4:24), took on humanity and mortality in the incarnation. That was essential, for neither animal blood nor the life of a sinful human could rescue the sinner. Only a divine sacrifice could do that. Therefore, he that was "existing in the form of God, counted not the being on an equality with God a thing to be grasped, but emptied himself, taking the form of . . . man" (Phil. 2:6), and offered himself on Calvary.

We can sing with S.J. Henderson, "Saved! saved! My sins are all pardoned, my guilt is all gone!"[1] No one under the Old Covenant could join in the song. They had promises of what would become true in later times. The Christian readers of Hebrews knew that hopes had turned into realities since Jesus had come. They needed to awaken to the realization that to leave Jesus and return to the temple with its priesthood and Old Covenant was to leave salvation. What animal sacrifice failed to provide, Jesus offered. To return from the fulfillment to only the picture was to turn from real water to but a desert mirage. Only those that turn to Christ and remain in Christ can join in the chorus, "Gone, gone, gone, gone! Yes, my sins are gone."[2]

At every Jewish Passover the lambs were sacrificed to roll the sins ahead another year. Israel understood that as interest payments may postpone paying off the debt, eventually the debt itself must be paid and paid in full.

THE MONARCHY IS BETTER

God of old time spoke through prophets. That word was good. Today God has "spoken unto us in his Son." This message from heaven is "better." Priests long ago made intercession for sinners. That ministry was helpful. Today Jesus has "made purification of sins." This mediation is "better." From Sinai on, Israel was the nation of God. That government was benevolent. After Jesus' atoning death and victorious resurrection, he "sat down on the right hand of the Majesty on high." The present monarchy of the church, God's new Israel, is "better." It can be said that as marvelous as was the Old, the New has brought us a higher plane. The message, the mediation and the monarchy go beyond what was known before.

The ancient prophets foresaw the time when a descendant of David would reign over the whole world and not just over Palestine. That hope fanned into a flame when God raised up the prophet John the Baptist. Since Malachi there had been a famine for the word of God. No prophet had spoken for four hundred years.

Finally John's voice broke the silence. The message was, "Repent ye; for the kingdom of heaven is at hand" (Matt. 3:2). God's reign was near. It was about to break in upon them. From one end of Palestine to the other, the people were on tip-toe. Jesus worked miracles, taught as no other, died, rose again and, after many appearances to his disciples, ascended to heaven where he "sat down on the right hand of the Majesty on high." Hebrews 1:3 speaks of Christ's coronation as King of kings.

Observe the contrasted monarchies. Israel's throne was in earthly Jerusalem. Jesus' throne is in the heavenly Jerusalem. It is a better throne. Earthly thrones pass away. The book of Hebrews was written in A.D. 68 or 69, just prior to the fall of Jerusalem which history records at A.D. 70. Any hope placed in the earthly Jerusalem would have been short-lived. The believer's King reigns forever on the imperishable throne of the abiding, eternal city of God. Such was the burden of Peter's sermon on the first day of the church. He reasoned that the descent of the Holy Spirit on that grand day was evidence that Jesus was now reigning as "Lord and Christ" (Acts 2:36).

The borders of the New Israel are not the Mediterranean Sea and the Jordan River — old Palestine. The New Israel does not have such limitations. The Messiah with "all authority . . . in heaven and on earth" (Matt. 28:18) orders the evangelistic conquest of "all the nations."

Under the Old Covenant, as recorded in the Old Testament Scriptures, there were many physical blessings promised to the Jewish nation. Today, as a New Testament preacher, I point you to the New Covenant promises. These spiritual promises are even better. Jesus promises his people remission of sins, the gift of the Holy Spirit and everlasting life. To suggest these few is just to hint at the many others to be found in the words of the Saviour and the writings of his apostles.

I have recently been crossing borders into foreign nations. To go behind the Iron Curtain made a border-crossing an unforgetable experience. Before you entered an East Germany, a Hungary or a Romania, you faced hours of questioning and possible inconveniences of car and baggage search. Only then were you permitted to cross that border. May I suggest that baptism is the border crossing into God's New Israel. It is the line between the kingdom of darkness and the realm of God's Son.

Learn about border-crossings. There can be many questions before you cross. In the case of Christianity there is only one question. It is, "Do you believe that Jesus is the Christ, the Son of the living God?" When a person decides to accept Christ as his Saviour, he is not drilled with a barrage of questions over a hundred different doctrines deemed important to some. The person is asked only if he or she believes in Jesus (cp. Acts 8:37).

Once a border is crossed you begin to see some differences. There is a language change, a money change, a cultural change. A restaurant just a few kilometers from the border may convince you that the foods of one country may differ from those so recently enjoyed that short distance before. At any border-crossing changes take place. That is intentionally true at baptism that separates between the world's realm and God's kingdom.

Upon entering the church, Christ's domain, one begins to talk differently. Different values are held. A lifestyle is not the same once on the other side of this line of demarcation. The book of Hebrews intends to remind the former Jews that had crossed over to Christ that what is now theirs is better, better, better. With no denigrating their former condition in Judaism, their present state in Christ's church is to be appreciated and retained. Good, better and best are comparative words. The best is in Jesus. All will go better for those who have decided for the best.

Endnotes

1. "Saved by the Blood" in *Favorite Hymns of Praise* (Wheaton, IL: Tabernacle Publishing Co., 1967), p. 329.
2. Helen Griggs, "My Sins Are Gone," *Youth Sings* (Mound, MN: Praise Book Publication, 1951), p. 85.

CHAPTER TWO

Be An Angel
Hebrews 1:4-14

(The Spreading of the Message)

To ask you to be an angel is not a request that you be an Angelino and move to Los Angeles, for you are needed where you are. Neither am I admonishing you to become an Angel fan and root for the baseball team that is based in Anaheim, California. Rather I place my appeal on Hebrews 1:14 that informs us that angels are "all ministering spirits, sent forth to do service for the sake of them that shall inherit salvation."

Nowhere in the Bible does one get the idea that at death a human being becomes a spirit being known as an angel. Humans and angels are two separate orders in God's creation. Yet, let me draw this implication. If angels minister for the sake of those that shall inherit salvation, is there not a part of that needed ministry we humans could do as well?

Take a quiz. When a man dies does he become an angel? The Bible answer is negative. How many angels are there? Revelation 5:11 replies, "I heard a voice of many angels round about the throne . . . and the number of them was ten thousand times ten thousand, and thousands of thousands." Hebrews 12:12 echoes that there are "innumerable hosts of angels." Are all angels alike? The Scripture responds "no." It speaks of cherubim, seraphim and even of archangels. But, now, hear the important question. It is not how many angels can dance on the point of a pin. It is, if angels are ministers of God, is there a way in our ministry that we can render some of the same acts of service? The answer is yes indeed! Check out my acrostic with your Bible.

BE AN ANNOUNCING ANGEL

It is Christmas time in your mind. Your heart begins to sing the words of Charles Wesley, "Hark! the herald angels sing, 'Glory to the new-born King.'" Your thoughts carry you to a hillside in Bethlehem where shepherds hear angels announce,

> Be not afraid; for behold, I bring you good tidings of great joy which shall be to all the people: for there is born to you this day in the city of David a Saviour, who is Christ the Lord. . . . And suddenly there was a multitude of the heavenly host praising God, and saying, Glory to God in the highest, And on earth peace among men in whom he is well pleased (Luke 2:11-14).

What had angels done? They had announced a wonderful fact regarding God's Son. What an important ministry!

BE AN ANGEL

When John the Baptist was about to be born, it was the angel Gabriel that told the good news to Zacharias the father (Luke 1: 11-20). The same angel brought the birth announcement of Jesus to the virgin Mary (1:26-38). It was an angel that instructed Joseph, "Thou shalt call his name Jesus; for it is he that shall save his people from their sins" (Matt. 1:20-21).

At the other end of the earthly life of Christ when his tomb was found empty by the women at dawn on that Sunday, it was an angel that was sent to herald the goodtidings, "Fear not ye; for I know that ye seek Jesus, who hath been crucified. He is not here; for he is risen. . . . Go quickly, and tell his disciples" (Matt. 28:5-7).

What can we conclude? There are times throughout the Bible when the ministry of angels was simply to announce facts of importance for the people of God. May I invite you to share in such a service? Be an announcer. Tell the story. There is power in words. Dial a friend. Tell him what a grand hour the worship service is at your church. Invite him to come with you. That kind of invitation can be angelic in the blessing it brings. Writing letters, speaking to neighbors and visiting homes are ministries with similarity to that of angels.

BE A NUDGING ANGEL

Allow me to explain what I mean by nudging angel. I have loved to read for many years the last page of the *Christian Century* magazine. That page was penned by the late Halford E. Luccock of Yale University under the pen-name Simeon Stilites. Each was a letter addressed to "St. John's down by the gas station." One such epistle questioned why we decorate Christmas trees with what we call "angel hair" because of its softness. He inquired why we sing the hymn "Whispering Hope" with its line, "Soft as the voice of an angel." Where, he wanted to know, did the idea come from that the words "angels" and "soft" ever belong together? He argued that in the Bible angels are more to be compared to a fire bell at 2:00 o'clock in the morning, or to an ambulance siren in the middle of the night. Acts 5 portrays an angel in the dark of the night startling the apostles awake, opening their prison doors and commanding, "Go ye, and stand and speak in the temple to the people all the words of this Life" (v. 19-20). That was a nudge from an angel.

You be an angel. Nudge someone. A little push is all many fellow-Christians need. They lack only an encouragement to act. When the apostles bogged down in their evangelistic assignment, asking, "Lord, dost thou at this time restore the kingdom to Israel?," Jesus nudged them back on track. He said, "It is not for you to know. . . . Ye shall be my witnesses" (Acts 1:6-8). Angels joined in the nudge of encouragement as Jesus began ascending heavenward. They addressed the apostles with, "Why stand ye looking into heaven?" (1:11). The angelic word was, "Don't spend your time 'gazing,' spend your time 'going' as instructed."

How like angels! They not only announce important information for the world to know, they nudge and encourage people to do their ministries. Every church needs more men like Barnabas. His name means "Son of exhortation" or "Son of encouragement" (Acts 4:36).

The author of Hebrews admonishes the people to "consider one another to provoke (encourage) unto love and good works . . . exhorting one another" (10:24-25). That is a call for nudging, if I ever heard one. Absentees would start attending again. All they require is a gentle nudge. People capable of teaching a class are ready to take on the needed service. They, too, but wait for the encouraging nudge. In some cases the youth sponsor slot, or nursery attendant vacancy will not get filled until, like an angel, we turn the soft nudge into a strong poke in the ribs. That is angelic too. Satan's strongest tool is discouragement. Angelic nudges overcome devilish doubts and demonic irresponsibility.

BE A GUARDING ANGEL

The "A" in angel is the invitation to announce God's message. The "N" in angel is the appeal to nudge Christians to render the service of which they are capable. The "G" in angel is the call to guard or protect the weak. That is a greatly needed ministry.

Do you believe in guardian angels? I know you have seen paintings that depict a child playing. In the background is a hovering angel protecting that child. Is that just a human opinion, or is it the teaching of the Bible?

In Matthew 18:10 Jesus warns, "See that ye despise not one of these little ones: for I say unto you, that in heaven their angels do always behold the face of my Father who is in heaven." We observe that Jesus speaks not of simply *"an* angel" but of *"their* angels." This appears to imply that each child has a particular angel assigned to him or her.

In another New Testament passage James has been killed with the sword and church is in prayer for imprisoned Peter. As they pray a knock is heard at the door. The servant girl, Rhoda, is sent to the door and she returns to announce that it is Peter. They say that she is "mad." Upon her unwavering insistence, they said, "It is his angel" (Acts 12:15). Again I invite you to note the words "*his* angel." That is saying more than just "*an* angel." Such a passage has led many to conclude that, as Peter was assigned to a special angel, so all of us have guardian angels from the time of our conversion.

We do know that the Bible pictures angels as guardian beings. Recall Daniel in the lion's den. He shouts to the king of Babylon, "My God hath sent his angel, and hath shut the lions' mouths, and they have not hurt me" (Daniel 6:22). Even Satan was aware of the angelic ministry of guarding. In the wilderness of temptation, he reminds Jesus of the promise in the book of Psalms, "He shall give his angels charge concerning thee: and, On their hands they shall bear thee up, Lest haply thou dash thy foot against a stone" (Matt. 4:6).

Do we need to share with angelic hosts the ministry of guarding God's people? I believe we must, for our "adversary the devil, as a roaring lion, walketh about, seeking whom he may devour" (I Pet. 5:8). Once a person has come out of the kingdom of darkness into the realm of light, Satan works all the harder to lure that individual back. We need to help guard and protect every lamb that is in our fold. No one of us can make it alone. If God has sent angels to announce, nudge and guard, there is no reason on the human side we can not share in such needed ministries.

BE AN EVANGELIZING ANGEL

The Greek word ἄγγελος, which we often transliterate "angel," means "messenger." Sometimes those who translated your English Bible used the word "messenger," when the subject was a human being. Yet they did not translate at all when a spirit being was under consideration. They only spelled the Greek word with English letters.

Take for instance the Isaiah prophecy applied in Mark 1:2 to John the Baptist. It reads, "Behold, I send my messenger before thy face, Who shall prepare thy way." John the messenger (angel) was a human evangelist. That is, he announced the good tidings of Jesus as a messenger.

When you gaze but a moment at the word *evangelist*, you see the word angel in the center of it. The letters "ev" or "eu" at the beginning of the word mean good. Hence the evangel is the good news and the evangelist the bearer of that glad message.

The spirit beings known as angels do not share directly in the task of evangelism. Their part is indirect. They may nudge a Philip to travel the road from Jerusalem to Gaza so that Philip might speak of Christ to an Ethiopian eunuch (Acts 8:26). The happy task of spreading the gospel throughout the world has been given to the church. It will not be reassigned to angels that stand ready to do God's bidding. When these ministering spirits come into the Biblical story, it is not to do some Christian's job for him. It is rather to get the proclaimer at his commissioned duty.

Wouldn't it be easier if the church could simply attend prayer-meetings and petition the Lord to save our world through angelic intervention? No line of the Bible hints that world-salvation will come that way. Heaven has legions of angels, but God has pre-determined that angels will not fulfill Christ's great commission. It is rather by the lips of men that have known forgiveness that the story of redemption is to be told. No fallen angel has ever known forgiveness. As Peter wrote, "God spared not angels when they sinned, but cast them down to hell (*Tartarus*), and committed them to pits of darkness, to be reserved unto judgment" (II Pet. 2:4). It is a different story regarding humans that fell into sin. They receive the gracious offer to have their iniquities covered and their sins forgiven. God has chosen the forgiven sinner as the messenger to bear the story of Christ's amazing grace to the other sinners.

Let me assert the fact again so that not one misunderstands. Angels exist. The Holy Spirit is everywhere. But neither God's Spirit nor his serving angels will ever directly turn a human heart from sin to salvation. The news that God saves sinners will be "made known through the church . . . according to the eternal purpose" (Eph. 3:11). Yet angels care about evangelism. Jesus said so. In his parable about finding the lost, he argued, "there is joy in the presence of the angels of God over one sinner that repenteth" (Luke 15:10). However, while angels care about soul-winning, it is humankind that does the work of evangelism. We the people can do that work. We must do that work or it will not be done.

BE A LAUDING ANGEL

To laud someone is to praise someone. One of the seven quotations about Christ's superiority to angels in Hebrews 1, reads, "And let all the angels of God worship him" (v. 6). From one end of the Bible to the other, humans are forbidden to bow down before, or to worship, an angel. Rather, with all the angels, we are invited to join in bowing before and worshipping Jesus Christ.

Such teaching makes clear that Jesus is no angel — no created being. In Revelation, the apostle John is rebuked for falling down to worship before the feet of an angel. "See thou do it not" was the angelic shout (22:9). The same book rather tells of heaven's myriads saying with a great voice, "Worthy is the Lamb that hath been slain to receive the power, and riches, and wisdom, and might, and honor, and glory, and blessing" (5:12).

It is a fitting ministry for all the saved to join in the praise of our Creator and Redeemer. If it is right for angels to laud God, how much more it is expected and right that forgiven men should join in their Maker's praise.

Before the world was created there were angels that rebelled against God. Not one of them was offered forgiveness. Each of them is pictured as bound with chains in eternal darkness awaiting the lake of fire. Fortunately, in the love of God, rebellious men upon repentance can receive unmerited forgiveness. Who could be so unresponsive to such grace that he would not join in the praise of his Saviour? It is our "spiritual service" (Rom. 12:2). It is our "reasonable worship."

CHAPTER THREE

So Great a Salvation
Hebrews 2:1-4

(The Greatness of the Message)

> Wonderful grace of Jesus, Greater than all my sin;
> How shall my tongue describe it, Where shall its praise begin?
> Taking away my burden, Setting my spirit free;
> For the wonderful grace of Jesus reaches me.
>
> Wonderful the matchless grace of Jesus,
> Deeper than the mighty rolling sea;
> Higher than the mountain, sparkling like a fountain,
> All-sufficient grace for even me,
> Broader than the scope of my transgressions,
> Greater far than all my sin and shame,
> O magnify the precious name of Jesus, Praise His name![1]

What a great salvation Jesus came to bring! It is something to sing about. And according to Hebrews, it is something to be warned about. Hear with open ears these words: "Therefore we ought to give the more earnest heed to the things that were heard, lest haply we drift away from them. For if the work spoken through angels proved steadfast, and every transgression and disobedience received a just recompense of reward; how shall we escape, if we neglect so great a salvation?" (Heb. 2:1-3).

Did you hear that unanswerable question, "How shall we escape, if we neglect so great a salvation?" To reject or neglect God's way of salvation leaves us with no other exit. God worked out but one way of salvation, the way through his Son. No other path to heaven is available.

Every criminal knows there are three ways of possible escape. You may escape being seen. Should that fail, and you are spotted in the act of committing a crime and the police begin to pursue you, you possibly might escape in a "revved up" car that could go faster than that of the law officer. And even if caught by a road-block and thrown into the brig, one yet might escape by bribing the jailer or master-minding a prison break.

None of this, however, would work with God. Be not deceived. We cannot escape being seen. God is omniscient. And being omnipresent there is nowhere to flee but what he is already there. It would be foolish to imagine that the Almighty could be over-powered or the Holy One be bribed. This leaves the unanswered question,

> How shall we escape, if we neglect so great a salvation? Which having at the first been spoken through the Lord, was confirmed unto us by them that heard; God also bearing witness with them, both by signs and wonders, and by manifold powers, and by gifts of the Holy Spirit, according to his own will. (2:3-4)

SO GREAT A SALVATION

SPOKEN BY THE GREAT MASTER

Let us consider the several points the inspired author of our epistle is making. Let us deal with them one at a time. This great salvation was first "spoken through the Lord."

Remember that day when four people so wanted their paralytic friend to receive Jesus' healing touch that they dug a hole through the roof of the crowded house where Jesus was teaching? When the Master saw the man being lowered on a sheet through the man-made opening, he responded to such faith. He uttered, "Son, thy sins are forgiven" (Mark 2:5). While salvation will be purchased later on the cross of Calvary, it earlier here was "first . . . spoken through the Lord."

One day a leper knelt before the Great Teacher and said, "If thou wilt, thou canst make me clean." The Lord responded, "I will; be thou made clean" (Mark 1:40-41). It was "first . . . spoken through the Lord."

They dragged the dishevelled woman before Jesus, charging that she had been caught in the very act of adultery. Hate gleamed in their eyes as they reminded Jesus of the law's demand for stoning. They taunted the benevolent Saviour with the dare, "What then sayest thou of her?" (John 8:5). At first he was quiet and stooped to write in the sand. Then he broke the prolonged silence, asking the "sinless" one in their midst to cast rock number one. After all had left self-condemned by inner guilt, the Lord inquired, "Woman, where are they? did no man condemn thee: go thy way; from henceforth sin no more" (John 8:1-10). It was first . . . spoken through the Lord."

It was dark as night when Nicodemus came to Jesus. That very hour this religious leader learned that even he must be born again to enter heaven's kingdom. Before they parted from one another the Pharisee heard from Jesus' lips the gospel:

> And as Moses lifted up the serpent in the wilderness, even so must the Son of Man be lifted up; that whosoever believeth in him may have eternal life. For God so loved the world, that he gave his only begotten Son, that whosoever believeth on him should not perish, but have eternal life. For God sent not the Son into the world to judge the world; but that the world should be saved through him (John 3:14-17).

It was "first . . . spoken through the Lord."

Jesus not only communicated the glad tidings privately to individuals, he often spread the gospel publicly. In the famous Sermon on the Mount, the Son of God told the multitudes that those who "hunger and thirst after righteousness . . . shall be filled" (Matt. 5:6). It was "first . . . spoken through the Lord."

In the upper room the One soon to be crucified took the emblems of bread and wine. He spoke regarding the cup, "This is my blood of the covenant, which is poured out for many unto remission of sins" (Matt. 26:28). It was "first . . . spoken through the Lord."

The Scribes and Pharisees drove him into a corner, murmuring that he was ever receiving and eating with sinners (Luke 15:2). That accusation drew out of Christ the beautiful parables about finding the lost. He said when a sheep is lost you search until you find it and return it to the fold. When a coin is lost you scour the house until it is restored to safe keeping. And when a son is lost in a far country, the Heavenly Father's heart knows the greatest of joys, when he sees the prodigal returning home. It was "first . . . spoken through the Lord."

SPREAD BY THE GREAT MESSENGERS

It was "first . . . spoken through the Lord" according to the author of Hebrews. Then he adds that the message of salvation "was confirmed unto us by them that heard." The reference now is to the apostles. While the writer and readers of the epistle to the Hebrews had never seen or heard Jesus in the flesh, they believed the information about him that had reached their ears by the apostles of Christ. The apostles were the witnesses that had walked the roads of Palestine with him. They were the ones whose eyes had seen his healings and whose ears had heard his sermons. They were the ones who announced his redeeming death and resurrection.

The men Jesus picked to be apostles were promised that God's Holy Spirit would guide them "into all the truth" (John 16:13) and bring to their "remembrance all that" was "said" to them (John 14:26). The risen Saviour called them his "witnesses" to bring the gospel story "unto the uttermost part of the earth" (Acts 1:8). Across the world they went telling the same great salvation that had first been spoken by the Lord.

We see Peter rise to his feet on the historic Pentecost of A.D. 30. The other apostles join him. The message is "whosoever shall call on the name of the Lord shall be saved" (Acts 2:21). The believers are counseled, "Repent ye, and be baptized everyone of you in the name of Jesus Christ unto the remission of your sins; and ye shall receive the gift of the Holy Spirit. For to you is the promise, and to your children, and to all that are afar off, even as many as the Lord our God shall call unto him" (2:38-39). This message was passed on and "confirmed . . . by them that heard."

Three thousand converts were not enough for Peter, so we find him preaching again by the beautiful gate of the temple in Jerusalem. This time the message is, "Repent ye therefore, and turn again, that your sins may be blotted out, that so there may come seasons of refreshing from the presence of the Lord" (Acts 3:19). Once again we see that the gospel story was passed on by those that heard. We did not get to live in that day and hear with our ears the oral testimony of the apostles. However their witness has reached us in the written form of Gospel and Epistles.

Scan the book of Romans and you are reminded that "the gospel . . . is the power of God unto salvation to every one that believeth; to the Jew first, and also to the Greek. For therein is revealed a righteousness of God from faith unto faith; as it is written, But the righteous shall live by faith" (1:16-17). We become aware that "being therefore justified by faith, we have peace with God through our Lord Jesus Christ; through whom also we have had our access by faith into this grace wherein we stand; and we rejoice in hope of the glory of God" (5:1-2). We learn that "there is therefore now no condemnation to them that are in Christ Jesus. For the law of the Spirit of life in Christ Jesus made me free from the law of sin and death" (8:1-2).

SUPPORTED BY THE GREAT MIRACLES

What was first "spoken through the Lord, was confirmed unto us by them that heard; God also bearing witness with them, both by signs and wonders, and by manifold powers, and by gifts of the Holy Spirit, according to his own will" (Hebrews 2:3-4). After the great salvation was spoken by the great Master and spread across the world by the voice and pen of the great messengers that we call apostles, what is this witness that God bears "with them?" Our inspired penman is pointing to the supportive miracles that accompanied the apostles' testimony. The "signs . . . wonders . . . manifold powers" and "gifts" were God's "amen!" to what his messengers said regarding his Son.

It is important to define what we mean by a miracle. Some people use the term rather broadly. My highly esteemed friend Carlton C. Buck wrote the popular hymn that goes, "I believe in miracles — I've seen a soul set free." The song continues, "I've seen the lily push its way up thru the stubborn sod — I believe in miracles, For I believe in God!"² That song is one of my favorite hymns, as Carlton is one of my special friends. However, that is not how I use the term miracle. Lilies have been pushing their way up through the sod since time immemorial. That is the way God normally operates in the universe He created.

To me the word miracle designates a situation where God works in a different way than usual to attract the attention of men. How do you account for three thousand converts on the one day of Pentecost? Jesus had "spoken" of the great salvation. The apostles had passed the message on to the hearers as recorded in Acts 2. But then, in addition, God worked a miracle that was convincing and supportive. These Galileans (the apostles) were enabled to talk in the native languages and dialects of the people who had come to Jerusalem from the many nations named both East and West, both North and South (Acts 2:5-11). They had not over the years mastered these tongues in classrooms or universities by working arduously at the task. Rather, instantaneously and perfectly "as the Spirit gave them utterance" (2:4), the apostles' lips spoke unhaltingly in each hearer's "own language" by miracle of God. The apostles were testifying, but so was "God also bearing witness with them."

On another day at the hour of prayer in the temple, a lame man is to be seen in his usual spot asking for alms. This well known beggar has been by that door for decades, as every sojourner to Jerusalem could testify. Yet on this particular day Peter says, "In the name of Jesus Christ of Nazareth, walk" (Acts 3:7). And there the former lame man stands, walks and leaps. He has been healed immediately and completely.

God always answers prayer. You know that from long experience. You this very week have known prayer to be answered. When God in His mercy begins a gradual healing in response to your intercession (sometimes through means, sometimes without means), the word miracle really does not fit. To be a miracle, an act by God must happen in a manner different from His usual way of working. This difference will catch man's attention, for the healing occurs instantly (rather than over time) and the recipient is perfectly whole (not just improving).

Rains begin to fall and the grape vine gradually begins to drink in the moisture. Over time that water becomes wine. That is the way God has always done it over the millenniums. Yet, at Cana of Galilee, in but a moment of time, the Lord spoke the word and water became wine instantly. God alone does it either way. But when He acts in the unique way it becomes a "sign" pointing to Christ (John 2:1-11). Here again the word miracle fits.

In the first century, as the apostles bore testimony to what they had seen and heard, that message was so credible because the witnesses' testimony on earth was confirmed by the divine miracle from above. No wonder the apostolic church grew so rapidly. Paul could remind the Corinthians that "the signs of an apostle were wrought" in their presence (II Cor. 12:12).

We use the word miracle where the Bible speaks of signs, wonders, powers and gifts of the Holy Spirit. A miracle is called a "wonder," for that is the effect produced upon its observers or readers. They stand in awe at the display of God's love and power. A miracle is defined as a "sign," for a sign on a street corner points to something. The miracles of Jesus and his chosen witnesses point like a signpost to the fact that the Lord is God's Son and the apostolic gospel is heaven's truth. The term "manifold powers" informs us that no human power could ever accomplish these benevolent deeds. Christ did miracles of every kind. They sprang from a word or a touch from Jesus and his men. Only the Holy Spirit's "gifts" could make possible what was impossible to humans.

Mark was right. The apostles "went forth, and preached everywhere, the Lord working with them and confirming the word by the signs that followed" (Mark 16:20). Jesus was a miracle worker. The prophet, John the Baptist, "did no sign" (John 10:4), but the Messiah he introduced did many mighty works. And the apostles Christ sent were commissioned to "heal the sick, raise the dead, cleanse the lepers, cast out demons" (Matt. 10:8). The Acts of Apostles reports that "many wonders and signs were done through the apostles" (Acts 2:43). Three thousand baptized believers had experienced forgiveness and been given the Holy Spirit. Yet it was "by the hands of the apostles . . . (that) many signs and wonders (were) wrought among the people" (Acts 5:12). As time goes on these apostles will lay hands on some others who will join them in extending this miracle ministry (cp. Acts 6:6,8). However, from Acts 1 through 5 the apostles are the channel of Christ's miracles. The apostles had the credentials of miracle because they were Jesus' ambassadors. As commissioned men they could claim, "We are witnesses of these things." They could add, "and so is the Holy Spirit" (Acts 5:32). Luke echoes here the author of Hebrews. The apostles witnessed to the salvation first proclaimed by Jesus. Then God also bore witness by the miracles of the Spirit as He willed. Such manifestations of power gave credence to the incredible story of God's love and salvation tendered to all who would believe.

SET ASIDE BY LITTLE MEN

Look carefully again at the words of our text,

Hebrews 2. It speaks of "the word spoken through angels." This is a reference to the ten commandments brought by angels to Moses at Sinai (cp. Acts 7:53; Galatians 3:19). The author observes that this law "proved steadfast, and every transgression and disobedience received a just recompense of reward" (Heb. 2:2). The Old Testament made it clear that no law breaker got away with violating heaven's commands. Each violator of the old covenant received condemnation. Let the recipients of the new covenant be reminded. If the old law that came through angels had to be obeyed, what about the greater revelation that came through Jesus, God's only Son? Dare we reject it? Dare we neglect it? Dare we but dally with it?

You knew man was given a free will. That is why wherever the gospel went some would believe and others reject the offer. The word of Christ was that whoever believed and was baptized would be saved and those rejecting would be condemned (cp. Mark 16:16). No one would be forced to accept the great salvation. So we recapitulate. Jesus has spoken. The apostles have spread the word. Heaven has confirmed the message. Now each person must make the great decision regarding it. There is no "escape" if we reject this great salvation offer.

But give heed to the fact that the word written in this text addressed to believers is not "reject," it is "neglect" (2:3). Even we who have accepted the gracious offer need to give "earnest heed . . . lest haply we drift away" (2:1). Some may reject to their damnation. Others may initially say "yes" and then carelessly "drift." These may cease to "assemble together" (Heb. 10:25). Like a fisherman whose boat is anchored in the strongly receding tide may fail to notice he is being pulled out to sea from the security of the shore, the Christian can drift with the tide until his soul is endangered. The question remains. How shall we escape if we let ourselves "drift away?" The answer is clear. There is no escape. Therefore, anchor in the gospel. Drift not from it. It is man's only hope.

Endnotes

1. Harold Lillenas, "Wonderful Grace of Jesus" in *Favorite Hymns of Praise* (Wheaton, IL: Tabernacle Publishing Co., 1967), p. 470. Copyright assigned to Hope Publishing Co.
2. *Youth Favorites* (Grand Rapids: Zondervan, 1963), p. 44.

CHAPTER FOUR

A Long Way to Paradise
Hebrews 2:5-18

(The History of the Message)

It's a long way to Paradise. It was a long way from creation to Christmas. It appears that it will be a long way from Calvary to the second coming. History will establish that the way has been long from paradise lost to paradise regained.

At the Christmas season believers in Christ see a tremendous difference between the fabled Santa Claus and the truth of Jesus' incarnation. If someone should ask how far it is from their city to your city, you recognize that can be considered a relative question. It could be that the distance is not long if you mean by plane or bus, but extremely far if you mean by foot.

In a trip one year around the world, I looked at the map to discover the distance from Bangkok, Thailand to Chaing Kham where the missionary lived that my wife and I had determined to visit. The map did not make it appear to be very far. But after we had flown in a small plane to Lampang and then ridden on top of the produce of a truck to Phayao and then had begun the forty-hour walk across rice paddies toward the communist border, I changed my mind to believe it's a long way from Bangkok to Chiang Kham.

How far is it from heaven to earth and from earth to heaven? That is the question Hebrews 2:5-18 addresses. How far is it from man's creation in the image of God, his fall and then his rescue and entrance into eternal glory? The author of Hebrews quotes the great Psalm, chapter eight, that tells us what man is and how God intended him to reign over the rest of creation (Heb. 2:5-8). He then observes that the time has not yet come that all is subjected to man, as was the Creator's intention. In other words, the writer is clearly aware that it is to be a long time from the day man was made until man becomes what God meant for him to be.

Hear the words from David: "When I consider thy heavens, the work of thy fingers, The moon and the stars, which thou hast ordained: What is man that thou art mindful of him? And the son of man, that thou visitest him?" (Psa. 8:3-4). The author of Hebrews quotes the next line to read, "Thou madest him a little lower than the angels" (Heb. 2:7).

When you look at an angel brilliant in his glory and mighty in his power, you feel that you are far below angels in importance. But the Bible is reminding you that in the intention of God you have been made but "a little lower than the angels." The Scripture continues to speak regarding mankind, "Thou crownedst him with glory and honor, And didst set him over the works of thy hands: Thou didst put all things in subjection under his feet" (Heb. 2:7-8).

We look around in our world and we do not yet find everything subject to him. That was true in David's day and in the day of the epistle's writing. It remains the case today. Not yet is everything subject to man. Before man's crowning with glory, there would have to be a Calvary. Before there could be the atoning death on Calvary there must be Christmas with its incarnation. From creation to coronation with the intervals of Christmas and Calvary would be a long, long time.

FROM CREATION TO CHRISTMAS

At the beginning man was made in the image of God. The Creator purposed that his Adam and Eve would live according to his righteous will. Yet, because man sinned there had to begin long preparations across the centuries of time to make ready for God to bring a Saviour into history through a virgin named Mary.

The Old Testament is the story of that history of salvation. Along with all the essential preparations was that of predictive prophecy. God raised up spokesmen who pre-announced the Messiah's coming. The over three hundred prophecies in the Law, Prophets and Psalms built hope in Israel that redemption was on its way.

Someone has suggested that Christmas was moving day for God. In store-fronts you have seen notices that after such-and-such a date the business will be found at a new location. We might say that after the first advent God in a special way now dwelt among men.

BEST OF ALL IS JESUS

What we call the Christmas story is not a pagan tale of a man being deified. It is the divinely-revealed record of the Bible that God entered human history. The hymn of Isaac Watts announces, "Joy to the world! the Lord is come. Let earth receive her King." Charles Wesley joins herald angels at the thought that "Mild He lays His glory by, Born that man no more may die."[1]

One poet, Joseph Clark, has challenged us to remember the eternal difference between the New Testament account of Jesus' birth and the Santa Claus tradition that captures center stage at the Christmas season. The poem pleads with us in these words:

> The birthday of the Lord draws near:
> The Day of Days of all the year:
> A day of hope and joy and cheer.
> Keep Jesus Christ in Christmas.
>
> Let no old Santa crowd Him out,
> With whiskers grey and body stout.
> He helps the world forget about
> The loving Christ at Christmas.
>
> The day is Christ's by right divine,
> A day no myth should undermine,
> A day when thought and deeds sublime
> Should keep the Christ in Christmas.
>
> When every message, every gift,
> Should in some joyous way uplift
> One's very thoughts, and make them drift
> To Bethlehem at Christmas.
>
> Give other things a minor place,
> But tell to men of every race
> The story of this day of grace—
> Of Christ their Lord on Christmas.

History divided time that day between B.C. and A.D. No other doctrine is worthy of more celebration than the advent of God into time and space. The incarnation is essential to the crucifixion and resurrection. We joyously remember and gratefully sing:

> Down from His glory, Ever living story,
> My God and Savior came, And Jesus was His name.
> Born in a manger, For His own a stranger,
> A man of sorrows, tears and agony.
>
> What condescension, bringing us redemption;
> That in the dead of night,
> Not one faint hope in sight,
> God, gracious, tender, Laid aside His splendor,
> Stopping to woo, to win, to save my soul.[2]

FROM CHRISTMAS TO CALVARY

The incarnation (Christmas) was essential to Calvary. Jesus was "made a little lower than the angels" (Heb. 2:9) that he might "taste of death for every man." The Hebrew author argues, that "since then children are sharers in flesh and blood, he also himself in like manner partook of the same; that through death he might bring to nought him that had the power of death, that is, the devil" (2:14). Yet, before there could be the atoning death of Jesus there was of necessity the preceding sinless ·life. He can help us as a "faithful high priest.... For in that he himself hath suffered being tempted, he is able to succor them that are tempted" (2:17-18).

It was even a long way from the stable in Bethlehem,

the many years in Nazareth, the three and a half years of ministry until he goes to the cross as God's lamb to expiate the world's sins.

When asked "What is the gospel?" the brief Pauline answer is "Christ died for our sins . . . was buried . . . and . . . hath been raised" (I Cor. 15:3-4). Such a gospel could never have been an event of history until first there had been the divine visitation.

If you want to see the real Christmas tree, look at the cross. It was on that tree that God's gift to the world was hung. As Jesus so descriptively explained it to Nicodemus, "and as Moses lifted up the serpent in the wilderness, even so must the Son of man be lifted up; that whosoever believeth in him may have eternal life" (John 3:14-15). We correctly call the following words the gospel in a nutshell. "For God so loved the world, that he gave his only begotten Son, that whosoever believeth on him should not perish, but have eternal life" (John 3:16).

Paul traced the long, long trail from eternity into time and from the cross-event to glory in Philippians. He speaks of Jesus "existing in the form of God." He writes of him emptying himself to become "man" and a "servant" at that. He tells not only of his "death," but of the agonizing "death of the cross." The end of the long trail was exaltation as every knee bows (2:5-11).

FROM CALVARY TO CORONATION

How far is it from the Garden of Eden where man fell to the Paradise of God where redeemed men will live forever? We have tried to grasp the millenniums of time that have passed as God has prepared humanity from man's creation to Christ's coming. It was no short, uneventful trip from the angelic announcement that Christ was born in Bethlehem to the angel's words at the empty tomb "He is not here; for he is risen, even as he said" (Matt. 28:6). Even today after two thousand years of Jesus' church seeking the lost as commissioned, we may have a way to go before the number to be redeemed will share the glory of heaven's crown.

Note again David's Psalm that foresaw "all things under his (man's) feet" (Psa. 8:6). The New Testament finds this not yet to be a fact. Hebrews 2:8 asserts, "But now we see not yet all things subjected to him." What has happened is that Jesus has come to earth and done what was essential for man's recovery. He did "taste of death for every man" that he might bring "many sons unto glory" (Heb. 2:9-10).

If we but put our trust in the "author" of our salvation, we can await with joy the Lord's return. At that time will be the promised resurrection, when man can share in all that humanity was intended to be.

Faith, repentance, confession and baptism are termed by many "the steps of salvation." What little steps we are asked to take toward the outstretched arms of a gracious Saviour! What giant strides the Eternal God has taken to make salvation's offer a reality! The Creator stepped out of eternity into time. He walked the trails of Palestine all the way to the cross. With his church he has covered the globe with the invitation for all to "take the water of life freely" (Rev. 22:17). He waits but for the right moment to "come again and receive" us to himself (John 14:3).

Should not God's long strides toward you start you taking the short steps toward his waiting arms? No message could be clearer than that brought by Jesus. No revelation of God's nature as loving redeemer could be found to parallel the truth brought by Christ. No story needs to be heard by people with shattered hopes more than the Christian gospel of salvation. The story of the cross is the greatest story ever told. Best of all is Jesus.

Endnotes

1. "Hark the Herald Angels Sing," *Favorite Hymns of Praise* (Wheaton, IL: Tabernacle Publishing Co., 1967), p. 81.
2. William E. Booth-Clibborn, "Down From His Glory" *Favorites No. 2* (Grand Rapids: Zondervan, 1946), p. 12.

PART TWO

Jesus, the Provider of God's Greatest Deliverance

CHAPTER FIVE

Half Way to Glory
Hebrews 3:1-19

(A Deliverance Greater Than the Divine Sabbath)

The Bible is a picture book. The Old Testament is more than commandments and ordinances. It is more than historical records of Israel's past. Some of its peoples, places, things and events picture Jesus' ministry and the Christian era.

When Christ's apostles studied their ancient Scriptures, they saw Jesus foreshadowed in "the law of Moses, and the prophets, and the psalms" (Luke 24:44). Jonah's three days and three nights in the belly of the big fish typified the Messiah's three days and three nights in the heart of the earth (cp. Matt. 12:40). The flood that separated Noah's family from the corrupt society of their past was a figure of baptism's cleansing power (cp. I Pet. 3:20-21).

Each article of furniture in the ancient tabernacle was picture-prophecy of the New Testament era. Did not the lambs that were sacrificed at the altar foreshadow Christ on the cross? Was not the laver, where the priests washed before entering the holy place, a type of baptism? Could not a comparison be made between the tabernacle's table, altar of incense, and candelabra and the church's communion, prayer, and teaching? Clearly the third and fourth chapters of Hebrews parallel the deliverance brought by Christ with that initiated by Moses and consummated by Joshua. Moses is featured in chapter three for he began Israel's exodus. Joshua in chapter four is pictured as the one who climaxed that rescue account. The Christian is to see his deliverance from sin in the Old Testament story of Israel's escape from Egyptian bondage. Canaan and its milk and honey were symbols of the heavenly rest at the end of a believer's struggle. The ancient literal stories had abiding spiritual truths for the modern reader. From our baptism that began our walk with the Lord up to our death that concludes our journey into glory, we have hardships in the wilderness of trial and temptation.

CROSSING THE SEA (BAPTISM)

What the Red Sea was for the Jews, Christian baptism is for us. It gets us started. We leave the bondage of sin and Satan as Israelites exited out of Egypt from Pharaoh's power. From then on faithfulness to our Saviour is the need.

Jesus "was faithful." Moses "was faithful" (Heb. 3:2,5). Let the follower of Christ "hold fast . . . firm unto the end" (2:6). Hebrews continues, "Let the partakers of Christ . . . hold fast the beginning of . . . confidence firm unto the end" (2:14) and not be "disobedient" losing all because of "unbelief" (2:18-19), as did that earlier generation of Jews.

Paul is the one who pointed out the parallel between Israel's crossing of the sea and believer's baptism. He wrote, "For I would not, brethren, have you ignorant, that our fathers were all under the cloud, and all passed through the sea; and were all baptized unto Moses in the cloud and in the sea." He adds, "Now these things were our examples." He uses the word type. He goes on to say, "They happened unto them by way of example; and they were written for our admonition, upon whom the ends of the ages are come" (I Cor. 10:6,11).

So Paul saw in the story of going through the Red Sea a picture of converts to Christ going through the waters of baptism. What a picture of conversion. Can you visualize the dilemma facing the Israelites when God ordered, "Go forward"? Behind them was the Egyptian army in hot pursuit. To the side were mountains they could not scale. In front of them was a vast sea of water. As they began their obedient march into the sea, the water separated and became a wall on either side. Above them was a cloud of water hiding them from Pharaoh's army. Underfoot was formerly damp sand. With water on either side, a cloud above and sand below they were totally immersed, or "baptized," unto Moses. As the soldiers pursued the children of Israel, the waters receded and left the wicked Egyptian army drowned beneath the wave, while God's people stood totally free on the other side.

Lesson? Baptism is a separating ordinance. On one side of the sea Israel belonged to Egypt and were under the Pharaoh. On the other side they were free men under God's theocracy. Let the baptized remember that they have changed leaders. Once slaves, they are now free in Christ. No longer are they to serve Satan. They are constituted God's people, a holy nation. They are on their way to glory.

Jesus was right, when "the Son shall make you free, ye shall be free indeed" (John 8:36). Paul was correct, "There is therefore now no condemnation to them that are in Christ Jesus" (Rom. 8:1). He was accurate when he spoke of believers being "baptized into Christ" (Gal. 3:26:27) and "into his death" (Rom. 6:3). Peter's inspired promise to those who responded to the gospel was that everyone "baptized . . . in the name of Jesus" would experience "remission of . . . sins" (Acts 2:38).

At the sea, Israel changed leaders and they changed lands. They also received new laws. Soon after their deliverance, the Ten Commandments were given at Mount Sinai to these freed men. God made covenant with them. On the tables of stone were inscribed the record of their deliverance, "I am Jehovah thy God, who brought thee out of the land of Egypt, out of the house of bondage" (Exod. 20:2). Then follow the laws by which God's freed people were now to live.

As day follows night in these New Covenant times, I begin at my baptism to follow Christ as Israel had followed Moses. I have committed myself to follow the new covenant regulations. Jesus has become my guide to direct me onward, as I head for the promised land.

CROSSING THE JORDAN (DEATH)

Go to the other end of the typological story. Under

HALF WAY TO GLORY

Joshua, forty years later, the wandering Jews crossed the Jordan River into Canaan. As the sea, under Moses' leadership, opened up for Israel to cross, the river Jordan, under Joshua, opened up for the Israelites as they went in to possess their permanent abode. Forty years of nomadic life was traded in for a permanent homeland. Tents were for the past. Houses with foundations were now to be theirs. Jerusalem would become the capital city. A permanent temple would replace the portable tent of wilderness days.

Have you seen the meaning of this type? Have you heard the words of the Negro spiritual lately?

"Swing low, sweet chariot. Comin' for to carry me home! . . . I looked over Jordan an' what did I see . . . A band of angels comin' after me, Comin' for to carry me home!"[1]

Christians have always seen the Jordan River as a type of death. At the point when our spirit leaves our body, the life of wandering is over. We go to settle down in that holy place where God is adored and worshipped forever.

The author of Hebrews later speaks of Abraham looking "for the city which hath the foundations, whose builder and maker is God" (11:10). Jesus had viewed heaven as the "Father's house" of "many mansions" (John 14:2). That is no two rooms and a bath; no puptent under a tree. That is a mansion in which to dwell eternally. Paul rejoices that after "our tabernacle be dissolved, we have a building from God, a house not made with hands, eternal, in the heavens" (II Cor. 5:1). With David we know that after "the valley of the shadow of death," we "shall dwell in the house of

Jehovah for ever" (Psa. 23:4-6).

CROSSING THE DESERT (TRIAL)

Now for a hard part of the story. It is good news that one can start at baptism, be forgiven and find rescue from the bondage of sin and Satan. It is grand and glad tidings that in the future our eternal hope will be realized and we can live forever in the "land beyond the river, that we call the sweet forever."[2] But what lies in between? What might be our lot for the next forty years? Look at the Bible story.

After Israel crossed through the sea and before they crossed the Jordan, they crossed the desert. "Desert" is not spelled with a double "s," meaning "dessert." Life may not be cookies, pies and ice-cream. It sometimes is desert. Hot! Dry! Arid!

A modern danger is the false gospel that, upon conversion to Christ, all will be peaches and cream and pie a la mode. Sometimes it does not work out that way. You have crossed the sea of your baptism and your sins are forgiven. You have the hope of heaven that lies beyond the Jordan of your death. Yet, life in this world can be rough and difficult. One person may meet discouragement and be tempted to despair. A desirable option may seem to be the taking of a detour from the way. Scripture tells of the freed slaves after a time longing for the leeks, onions and garlic they had known before deliverance. There was a certain kind of security being under the dictatorship of Pharaoh. Freedom had its sweetness, but with it came responsibilities and hardships.

HALF WAY TO GLORY

It takes character to be Christian. There is no promise of an easy road for the ones who choose to follow Jesus. This should be no surprise. The New Testament Gospels tell of Jesus' baptism. You know what came next. It was the temptation in the wilderness.

Now look at our text, the letter to the Hebrews. It was an epistle written in the days when Nero was Emperor of Rome. Christians were being killed for only claiming to be a follower of Christ. So the author pleads with the believers to be faithful and hold fast. He reminds them that they are crossing the desert. He pleads, "Harden not your hearts, as in the provocation. Like as in the day of trial in the wilderness" (3:8).

The writer reminds the readers of the "forty years" when God was "displeased" (3:9-10). A straight line from Egypt to Canaan would not have taken forty days. Their route of wandering took forty years. It was a time of trial and testing. It was a period during which the genuineness of their faith could be tried. At the time they had been baptized in cloud and sea, were they ready to follow God all the way?

Paul knew the hardships that went with the gospel. He had been shipwrecked, beaten with rods, imprisoned and driven from synagogues and cities. His fellow apostles knew to expect martyrdom as the Old Testament prophets before them had been sacrificed. His Lord had gone the way of the cross. It is not in the tradition of Biblical faith to turn aside. It is right to call all those who have begun the race to continue. Beware of "falling away from the living God." Rather, "exhort one another day by day" to remain "firm unto the end" (3:12-14).

BEST OF ALL IS JESUS

Prior to the battle of the Alamo, Colonel Travis gathered his men inside the fort. He said, "Gentlemen, tomorrow General Santa Ana will be marching against us with twenty-five hundred men. We have but a handful left." He took his sword and thrust it into the dirt marking a long line from one end of the fort toward the other. He began speaking again to his soldiers, "If you love Texas more than you love life, more than you love your families at home; if you love your country, step across this line. Volunteer to fight until death."

History tells that General Santa Ana did march the next day against the Alamo. Every defender died but the one who escaped to tell this story. He related how at the time Colonel Travis had called for volunteers to cross the sword-drawn line, every man, but one, immediately stepped across it. The exception was Colonel Bowie, after whom the Bowie knife has been named. He was on a cot, so weak from loss of blood that he could not move himself. But, he could speak. He simply requested, "Will two men come back and get me?" Two men went back across the line, picked up their comrade's cot and brought him to their side. They all unitedly had made the courageous and costly decision.

To Paul, baptism was a kind of line between the world and the church. He knew God worked with the hearts of men before their baptisms. Had the Lord not so labored for the lost, there would have been no converts. Yet, he saw that when they came to the waters of baptism they had made a commitment. Aware as they were that rough might be the way, nevertheless, they had decided to cross the line and be marked as citizens in God's Church, the best of all fellowships.

Endnotes

1. *Twice 55 Community Songs* (Boston: C.C. Birchard and Company, 1917), p. 48.

2. Dion De Marbelle, "When They Ring the Golden Bells" *Favorite Hymns: An All Purpose Song Book* (Cincinnati: Standard Publishing Co., 1933), p. 63.

CHAPTER SIX

The Sabbath That Remains
Hebrews 4:1-11

(A Deliverance Greater Than the Divine Sabbath)

Does this phrase surprise you? "There remaineth therefore a sabbath rest for the people of God" (Heb. 4:9). Time and again you have heard that the sabbath was for Old Testament times and not for the church age. Had not Hosea prophesied, "I will also cause all her mirth to cease, her feasts, her new moons, and her sabbaths" (2:11)? How can the writer of Hebrews speak of a sabbath that remains? Paul told the Colossians that Christ had "blotted out the bond written in ordinances . . . nailing it to the cross" (2:14). He drew the conclusions that Christians ought not let anyone judge them regarding "a feast day or a new moon or a sabbath day." He spoke of these as but "a shadow of the things to come" (2:16-17). Yet, our Hebrews passage still claims there is a sabbath that remains.

Students of history find evidence of Christians meeting on the first day of the week in the writings of early Church Fathers. Eusebius, Ignatius, Justin Martyr, the Didache and other witnesses tell of Sunday assemblies, calling the first day of the week the resurrection day. But, Hebrews 4:9 still cries out, "There remaineth . . . a sabbath rest for the people of God."

The birthday of the church was not on a Saturday. God's kingdom began on a Sunday according to Acts 2:1. A quick comparison with Leviticus 23:15-16 makes that fact clear. God's Holy Spirit was sent by the Risen Christ to indwell his church on the first day of the week. Still, the text before us reasons that there is a sabbath that remains.

When did the earliest Christians, under apostolic guidance, meet for the Lord's Supper? Luke tells of such an assembly "upon the first day of the week" (Acts 20:7). When did the early church gather the offering? Paul's instruction to all his converts was, "Upon the first day of the week let each one of you lay by him in store" (I Cor. 16:2). The Greek of the last passage is strong to suggest that every first day, every believer was to share as he had prospered. However, Hebrews 4:9 is not to be quieted, as it argues there is a sabbath that remains.

Let's talk about this awhile. Sabbath means rest. The word "sabbath" is found a dozen times in the third and fourth chapters of Hebrews. It is unmentioned, however, in both its earlier and its later chapters. But it is found twelve times in these two chapters. Chapter 3 tells what Moses did. Chapter 4 speaks of what Joshua did. Then it adds what Jesus had accomplished. The key word of the book, "better," again comes into play. The rest Jesus offers is better. Moses brought a rest to the people of God. Joshua brought a rest to the people of

God. Now Jesus has brought the better rest. It is far more than the sabbath day. It is much superior to the rest from wandering given through Joshua. Jesus offered a rest of soul that is essential to all.

DAY OF REST

A sabbath rest did come through Moses. After the exodus Moses ascended Mount Sinai and God gave to him the ten commandments. How they begin you well remember, "I am Jehovah thy God, who brought thee out of the land of Egypt, out of the house of bondage. Thou shalt have no other gods before me" (Exod. 20:2-3). The fourth of the commands was,

> Remember the sabbath day, to keep it holy. Six days shalt thou labor, and do all thy work, but the seventh day is a sabbath unto Jehovah thy God: in it thou shalt not do any work, thou, nor thy son, nor thy daughter, thy man-servant, nor thy maid-servant, nor thy cattle, nor thy stranger that is within thy gates (Exod. 20:8-10).

What a grand day was the seventh-day sabbath. Every Israelite had been a slave in the land of Egypt. They had never known time off from work nor a forty-hour week. An eight-hour workday was not in their experience. Once God made these slaves free men, he called upon them to "remember" they were now his children. As sons of heaven's king, they were not to work, work, work, and never rest. They were now children of dignity. "Remember the sabbath day" was God's instruction. So sabbath after sabbath, seventh-day after seventh-day, down through the centuries, the nation of Israel remembered to whom they belonged.

When a Jew would have a Passover meal, he would not act like a slave and stand, while gulping down some food to keep body and soul together. He would recline at table on his left elbow. He was a free man. He and his would dine at leisure, remembering that their God had liberated them and made them a kingdom of priests.

As we speak of putting on "our Sunday best" as we go to church, the Jews would dress in the finest they had for their sabbath assembly. Not that clothing was all that mattered, but even their attire reminded them that they were sons of God. They were children of the King.

We sing,

> My Father is rich in houses and lands, He holdeth the wealth of the world in His hands! Of rubies and diamonds, of silver and gold, His coffers are full, — He hath riches untold. I am the child of a King, The child of a King! With Jesus my Savior, I'm the child of a King[1]

You can come to worship on the Lord's day clad any way you choose and you will be welcome. But, it is no accident that through the years people have dressed the neatest they could. It helped them remember that, in a world that may ignore or mistreat them, they belonged to God. By dress they were helped to remember their identity.

The sabbath was a wonderful day of rest. But Psalm 95 is then quoted by the author of Hebrews. There God warns, "They shall not enter into my rest" (Heb. 3:11). The Psalmist knew the seventh-day sabbath. For the forty years of wandering after Egypt, the Jews rested on

Saturday. Yet, there was coming a rest they would not enter. In chapter 4 the Hebrew writer quotes the warning again in verse 3. He refers to the seventh-day in verse 4. He seems to be speaking of the value of the sabbath observance that marked Jewish history, but stressing a needed rest that is far above the sacred day.

Have you noted that the fourth commandment not only called for rest on the seventh-day, but also for working the remainder of the time. "Six days shalt thou labor," were God's words to his people. Humans need constructive things to do. Jesus was a carpenter. Paul was a tent maker. The Saviour said, "My Father worketh until now, and I work" (John 5:17). There is dignity in toil. Working with one's hands is honorable. We are encouraged to "be steadfast, unmovable, always abounding in the work of the Lord, forasmuch as ye know that your labor is not vain in the Lord" (I Cor. 15:58). To make things with one's hands is to be sons of the Creator. To do things and accomplish tasks goes with being a follower of him who went about doing good. Back in the garden of Eden, before the fall, Adam worked the soil. What sin brought in was the sweat of the brow to the point that it became slavery and a burden.

To do constructive work throughout a week and to rest on the seventh day was a constant reminder of God's rescue of His people from slavery. Israel was instructed, "And thou shalt remember that thou wast a servant in the land of Egypt, and Jehovah thy God brought thee out thence by a mighty hand and an out-stretched arm: therefore Jehovah thy God commanded thee to keep the sabbath day" (Deut. 5:15). The sabbath was observed by Israel in remembrance that they once were slaves but now were free by the intervention of God.

LAND OF REST

Ever since they were constituted a nation at Mount Sinai, the Jews had the sabbath day, while they wandered for forty years through the wilderness. They knew they had been given a rest of a kind, but they needed more. What Moses had brought was the weekly sabbath day. What Joshua would bring would be the promised land and the end to their wanderings. He would lead them in the conquest of Canaan. From then on each man could have his own vine, fig tree and home. Each man would have a place to anchor.

Humans need this kind of rest as well. Every person ought to have a regular day of rest. He or she also longs for a place to settle down and call home. Even the sailor that sails the seven seas anticipates returning to his home port. The retirees, who love to travel, still look forward to returning home again.

Believers have learned that being a Christian-at-large lacks the blessing of having a home church. In the New Testament it would be difficult to find a follower of Jesus arguing that he belonged to the church universal, while denying a connection to the other believers in his home town. We all need a home church — a home base. It is not ideal to wander from church to church and from sect to sect.

To belong to Christ is good. The Bible reveals that each early believer belonged, as well, to Jesus' body, the church in his community. There are New Testament commands that can not be obeyed by those disconnected from the local body. Consider the selection of elders and deacons. That task was given to local churches. In Jerusalem the church was asked to select men "full of the Spirit and of wisdom" (Acts 6:3). How can shepherds tend a flock when they do not know who the particular sheep are that have been entrusted to their care (cp. Acts 20:28)?

We need a place to settle down. We need to be a part of a local family and share mutual ministries and responsibilities. To enjoy a day of rest and to have a place you call your own is a delight. One also needs to anchor down in apostolic teaching. Fellowship-wise, I draw no lines. I reach out to Catholics or Protestants who call Jesus their Lord. If they call themselves liberal or conservative, I overlook their labels and rejoice that they know of Jesus and claim allegiance to him. Yet, the local congregation to which I belong covenants to abide by the teaching of Christ as given to the church through his chosen apostles. I can anchor there. I know that at every assembly only Christ will be preached. There, all the Bible will be believed. There, nothing knowingly will be added, subtracted or changed from the practice of the earliest church.

ETERNITY OF REST

The burden of our text, Hebrews 4:1-11, is that we need a day of rest. We also require a salvation from wandering. All believers need to be rescued from being spiritually nomadic, wandering from doctrine to doctrine and from church to church. It is satisfaction to the soul to "search the Scriptures" and to settle down in unadulterated New Testament teaching. In addition, our passage in Hebrews calls for a further rest. It says, "If Joshua had given them rest, he would not have spoken afterward of another day. There remaineth therefore a sabbath rest for the people of God" (4:8-9).

This means that there remains one more rest yet to be given. The recipients of this epistle knew what the sabbath day was. Their people had kept the sabbath ever since the law was given at Sinai. They knew what the holy land was. Palestine had been theirs ever since the conquest under Joshua. But, that great Old Testament leader had not given them the rest that every sinner must have. Jesus alone brings that.

The superiority of Christianity to Judaism is the theme of the epistle before us. The Jewish Christians are informed that only to have what came in Old Testament days was not to have enough. In the Law and Prophets was but type and shadow. Jews had the sabbath day. Jews still had, at the writing of this letter, the holy land. Two years later that land would be no longer theirs and they as a people would be driven out. The one rest that was essential was that which follows from the remission of one's sins. Moses was used of God to bring freedom from slavery. Joshua was God's emissary to bring deliverance from wandering. Jesus came as God's mediator to offer salvation from sin, which promised eternal fellowship with God.

Listen to the Saviour speak with outstretched arms, "Come unto me, all ye that labor and are heavy laden, and I will give you rest. Take my yoke upon you, and learn of me; for I am meek and lowly in heart: and ye shall find rest unto your souls" (Matt. 11:28-29). The Master is addressing sabbath observers in the holy land. They, like we, did not have rest from a guilty conscience. They yet lacked rest of the soul.

Many years ago in the Northeast part of Portland, Oregon, lived a blind lady by the name of Mary Harding. She had Bible studies regularly in her home that attracted many ministers. This is one of the many poems she penned. It is her interpretation of Jesus' invitation:

"Come unto me," the Saviour said,
"and I will give you rest.
Thy heart I'll free from sin and dread
and guide thee for the best."

"I take thy rest, O Christ of God,
forgiveness from all sin.
For Thou hast shed Thy precious blood
deep peace to give within."

"Come weary, heavy-ladened heart,
cast all thy cares on me.
Peace to thy soul shall not depart
but last eternally."

"I cast my every care on Thee
in confidence sublime,
knowing that Thou wilt care for me
through all the years of time.

Nor will time end Thy care.
Thy fellowship but love divine
shall still be ours in heaven above
and all the glory Thine."

This poet was blind physically but she had clear insight. Jesus is the giver of the rest sinners need. It is not a day, nor a land, but an inward peace and an eternal promise. Such calm is the fruit of Christ's Spirit. He invites all to find that rest, which is the forgiveness of sin. He asked that "repentance and remission of sins . . . be preached in his name unto all the nations" (Luke 24:47). His command to the apostles was to start the proclamation "from Jerusalem." Obediently they announced in that city the promise that repentance and baptism in Christ's name would result in "remission of . . . .sins" (Acts 2:38). Even a person with a day off and his own home still needs the forgiveness that gives access to the eternal mansions.

Sing afresh the old hymn "Beulah Land." "I've reached the land of corn and wine, And all its riches freely mine . . . I look away across the sea, Where mansions are prepared for me, And view the shining glory-shore, My Heav'n my home, for-ever-more!"[2]

If you only have an earthly home, in a few years there will be a funeral and that old house will be yours no longer. But, if you have the total forgiveness of Christ, you will one day be on that glory shore. Heaven will be your home for-ever-more. Christ is the only way to heaven. He is "the way, and the truth, and the life: no one cometh unto the Father" (John 14:6) except through him.

Hebrews 4 is the plea to Jewish Christians not to "come short" (4:2) of Christ's rest. It is a warning against "disobedience" (4:6). It is an encouragement to stay by Christ until life is over and heaven has begun. The words are, "he that hath entered into his rest hath himself also rested from his works, as God did from his (4:10). The Bible's last book echoes this hope as the voice from heaven says, "Blessed are the dead who die in the Lord from henceforth: yea, saith the Spirit, that they may rest from their labors; for their works follow with them" (Rev. 14:13).

When we cross the Jordan of our death, we will enjoy the kind of rest God calls "his rest." "God rested on the seventh day from all his works" (Heb. 4:5). The point is that all the creating was done in the six days. On the seventh day, since God was completely through creating, he rested. When we enter into his rest — heaven — it will be when all our work on earth is finished. Weekly rest days but hint at the great rest that will come when all life's "labors and trials are o'er." Other rests are refreshing, but best of all is that brought by Jesus.

Endnotes

1. Hattie E. Buell, "The Child of a King," *Favorite Hymns: Number Two* (Cincinnati: Standard Publishing Co., 1942), p. 88.
2. Edgar P. Stites *Favorite Hymns of Praise*, (Wheaton, IL: Tabernacle Publishing Co., 1967), p. 481.

CHAPTER SEVEN

Piercing Sword or Protective Shield
Hebrews 1:12-16

(A Deliverance Grounded in Human Choice)

There are some things we don't know. There are other things we know with certainty. We do not know for sure who wrote the book of Hebrews. Some believe the epistle was penned by Paul. Others suggest Apollos as the author. Origen claimed that only God knew who its author was.

While we may not know who wrote this inspiring book, there is no doubt concerning what the author believed about his Old Testament Bible. He affirms: "The word of God is living, and active, and sharper than any two-edged sword." He sees it to be "piercing even to the dividing of soul and spirit, of both joints and marrow." He knows that word to be "quick to discern the thoughts and intents of the heart" (Heb. 4:12). As to the Scripture's inspiration and power, the author of Hebrews has no doubts. What does this New Testament writer have to say about the Son of God? He adds:

Having then a great high priest, who hath passed through the heavens, Jesus the Son of God, let us hold fast our confession. For we have not a high priest that cannot be touched with the feeling of our infirmities; but one that hath been in all points tempted like as we are, yet without sin. Let us therefore draw near with boldness unto the throne of grace, that we may receive mercy and may find grace to help us in time of need (Heb. 4:14-16).

Whoever was the penman of this passage, he was absolutely correct. We have a Word of God that is going to judge us, unless we accept the Son of God who stands ready to shield us from condemnation. The human race has but the option of condemnation under God's Word or salvation under God's Son.

Jesus' great commission promised, "He that believeth and is baptized shall be saved." It also warned, "He that disbelieveth shall be condemned" (Mark 16:16). The alternatives were clear. In the words of the forerunner, John the Baptist, the coming Messiah would "baptize . . . in the Holy Spirit and in fire" (Matt. 3:11). Again the world was reminded of its alternatives. Men would either be taken like valuable wheat into the garner of heaven, or they would be thrown like chaff into the burning flames at the end of history (cp. Matt. 3:12). For all people there is the choice of the heavenly Jerusalem or the garbage dump outside its gates. Will we be under the piercing sword of judgment, or under the protective shield of grace?

WORD OF GOD

God's Word, according to the text, is "living." The

PIERCING SWORD OR PROTECTIVE SHIELD

Scripture is not a dead letter. It is alive. As surely as Jehovah is "the living God" (Heb. 3:12), His revelation is both "living and active" (4:12). The Greek word for active is ἐνεργής, or energetic and full of power and vitality. If any person has been in trespass and sins, he must be "begotten again, not of corruptible seed, but of incorruptible, through the word of God, which liveth and abideth" (I Pet. 1:23).

Sitting one day in a jail in Rome, Paul spoke to Philemon's run-away slave, Onesimus. The powerful gospel turned the prisoner's life around. The apostle sent the now Christian slave back to his owner, calling Onesimus, "my child, whom I have begotten in my bonds" (Phile. 10). Once again the gospel proved to be the power to transform and save. The message spoken was "living and active." It pierced the heart of the runaway with convicting and converting power.

The same Paul, writing to the Corinthians many years before, spoke similarly: "though ye have ten thousand tutors in Christ, yet have ye not many fathers; for in Christ Jesus I begat you through the gospel" (I Cor. 5:14).

Hear this! Without the new birth we cannot "see" or "enter into the kingdom of God" (John 3:3,5). It is as if the heart of man is a womb. The seed of the word of God impregnates faith in the heart. Jesus explains, "The seed is the word of God" (Luke 8:11). The hearer of the gospel message finds faith conceiving in his innermost being. The living, active seed planted in the heart that is open to receive it, produces belief. That faith grows and develops and baptism follows. Hence the believer is born of both "water and the Spirit" (John 3:5).

That living, active word of God is also sharp and piercing. The first day that the gospel was preached as accomplished fact was in Jerusalem on the day called Pentecost. Three thousand responded to Peter's sermon because "they were pricked in their heart" (Acts 2:37). That means "the sword of the Spirit" (Eph. 6:17) had cut through. Consciences had been touched. Under conviction they surrounded Peter asking the way of salvation.

This piercing of conscience by the message should have been expected. The Messiah had told his followers that the promised Holy Spirit would be aiding them. He defined the Spirit's ministry, saying, "he . . . will convict the world in respect of sin, and of righteousness, and of judgment" (John 16:8).

In John's book of Revelation Jesus is symbolically pictured as having "feet like unto burnished brass" and "eyes . . . as a flame of fire" (1:14-15). Christ can look right within a person. He can know what each one is thinking. He can bring conviction.

The book of Hebrews exalts the revelation in God's Bible. Its writer praises that word as living, active, sharp, and piercing and capable of discerning our innermost thoughts. Do other New Testament writers agree? How do Peter, Paul, John or Jesus speak of the ancient writings of Moses and the prophets?

Jesus, the Lord of the church, referred to his Bible saying, "The Scripture can not be broken" (John 10:35). How much confidence did he want his disciples to place in the ancient writings? Christ's answer was, "Till heaven and earth pass away, one jot or one tittle shall in no wise pass away from the law till all things be accomplished" (Matt. 5:18). "Heaven and earth shall pass

PIERCING SWORD OR PROTECTIVE SHIELD

away," he added, "but my words shall not pass away" (Matt. 24:35). Christ's words have passed into poetry and music. They have passed into laws and proverbs. But they have not passed away.

Peter had the same confidence in Scripture that marked his Master. He declared no prophecy of scripture to be "of private interpretation." He reasoned that "no prophecy ever came by the will of man: but men spake from God, being moved by the Holy Spirit" (II Pet. 1:20-21). The fisherman knew it to be "the Spirit of Christ which was in them," as the old prophets "testified beforehand the sufferings of Christ and the glories that should follow them" (I Pet. 1:11). To Peter, his Bible was not the word of man about God. It was God's word directed to man.

If you had asked Paul whether he taught his personal opinions or a heaven-sent message, the answer would ring clear. Referring to his teachings, he claimed, "Unto us God revealed them through the Spirit. . . . Which things also we speak, not in words which man's wisdom teacheth, but which the Spirit teacheth, combining spiritual things with spiritual words" (I Cor. 2:10,13). Does he not mean that God has provided both the thoughts and the words by which to convey the ideas? The Thessalonians were commended by the apostle for recognizing the source of his preaching. He wrote, "And for this cause we also thank God without ceasing, that when ye received from us the word of the message, even the word of God, ye accepted it not as the word of men, but, as it is in truth, the word of God" (I Thess. 2:13).

Why are we reiterating what the Bible says about itself? Because we also read of church leaders today rewriting liturgy and Scripture to delete what they term its sexist language or its cultural biases. If the church at its beginning asserted, "Every scripture inspired of God is also profitable for . . . correction" (II Tim. 3:16), should not the modern church correct its opinions by the Bible rather than correct God's Bible by their opinions? Those who stand behind the pulpits of the churches ought never have to be asked if they believe the Scriptures. No question should be necessary regarding the preacher's beliefs about the virgin birth, the blood atonement or resurrection. That should be a foregone conclusion. The sacred desk should always have behind it a man certain about the Christ he preaches and the book containing that story.

Any church interested in restoring Biblical faith and practice, must know it has a dependable Bible. Human creeds can constantly be changed to match the mood of the hour. But a divinely given revelation bears the stamp of timelessness. The eternal gospel, like its author, is "the same yesterday and today, yea and for ever" (Heb. 13:8). Since God has condescended to reveal His will to man, it is vital that His messengers "speak where the Scriptures speak and be silent where they are silent." Congregations in the restoration tradition always have said, "We have no name but the divine name. We have no creed but Christ. We have no book but the Bible." We will strive never to add to its revelation nor alter its meaning. As John warned in the Bible's last book, "If any man shall add . . . God shall add unto him the plagues . . . and if any man shall take away . . . God shall take away his part from the tree of life, and out of the holy city" (Rev. 22:18-19).

SON OF GOD

Follow the writer of Hebrews as he moves from speaking of "the word of God" (4:12-13) to his comments regarding "the Son of God" (4:14-16). The word of God will condemn those that reject its message, which is the Son of God.

This Son of God is the "great high priest, who hath passed through the heavens, Jesus" (4:14). As earthly high priest on the Day of Atonement, he went from the temple's holy place to the most holy place. Passing from the forepart of the temple into the holy of holies, he passed through the veil. Behind that veil he could no longer be seen. That action became a typical picture of Jesus Christ who passed from the earthly scene into the heavens. The cubical holy of holies was the type of heaven itself, "the city . . . foursquare" (Rev. 21:16). One day Jesus will return from heaven as the Old Testament high priest came again from the holy of holies into the view of the people waiting for him.

In the interim, until Christ returns, we have not "a high priest that cannot be touched with the feeling of our infirmities; but one that hath been in all points tempted like as we are, yet without sin" (4:15). That is good news.

When you and I are tempted, we know that Jesus sympathizes. Every temptation we face, the Lord faced. This is the great fact of the incarnation. Prior to that, man might think God could not understand. Now that Jesus has come in human form, people should realize he knows what temptation is like. He did not yield to sin's lure. He can help us. He understands.

For this reason, "Let us therefore draw near with boldness unto the throne of grace, that we may receive mercy, and may find grace to help us in time of need" (4:16). The author of Hebrews so admonished his readers. What did Jesus say? Those in the upper room at the last supper saw him offer the cup to them with words of invitation, inviting, "Drink ye all of it; for this is my blood of the covenant, which is poured out for many unto remission of sins" (Matt. 26:27-28). He later admonished "that repentance and remission of sins should be preached in his name unto all the nations" (Luke 24:47). What the Saviour said to the woman taken in the act of adultery, he will say to any sinner: "Neither do I condemn thee: go thy way; from henceforth sin no more" (John 8:11). It can not be made plainer than Jesus made it to Nicodemus: "God sent not the Son into the world to judge the world; but that the world should be saved through him" (John 3:17).

What Jesus taught during his earthly ministry, his followers passed on in theirs. To Paul, sin's wages were seen to be death but God's free gift in Christ was known to be eternal life (cp. Rom. 6:23). John reminds his flock, "If any man sin, we have an advocate with the Father, Jesus Christ the righteous: and he is the propitiation for our sins; and not for ours only, but also the whole world" (I John 1:1-2).

What can we conclude? The Scriptures contain good-news and bad-news. The bad-news is that the Word of God speaks of transgressors being condemned eternally. But wait! There is good-news. There is a protective shield from God's judgment. That shield from condemnation is Jesus, the Son of God. "There is . . . now no condemnation to them that are in Christ Jesus" (Rom. 8:1).

One day I was giving lectures at San Jose Bible College. During a break I was seated with friends in the school's cafeteria. Not far away at that very moment Livermore, California, was the center of a sizable earthquake. Its strong tremors were felt in San Jose. As we sat drinking coffee the room started to shake and the chandeliers began to swing back and forth. Even the window drapes were in motion. My mind recalled that it would be appropriate to get under a table. But, looking up I saw directly above a huge, sturdy beam. This was likely the safest place in the building, so we opted to sit it out.

As Sol Hoopii wrote so long ago:

> When Jesus comes this earth will shake and hearts will quake.
> Be ready.
> When Jesus comes His face we'll see eternally.
> Be ready.
> Has your soul been filled with God's love and Holy Ghost?
> Are you saved and ready to meet the Lord of hosts?
> When Jesus comes, don't hesitate, don't be too late.
> Be ready.[1]

Unequalled is the message Jesus brought. Unparalleled is the deliverance he offered. Without peer is he who is best of all. The good being proclaimed by other voices is drowned out by the better that came from his lips.

Endnotes

1. Source unknown.

PART THREE
Jesus, the Offerer of God's Holiest Intercession

CHAPTER EIGHT

A Priest That Is Different
Hebrews 5:1-10

(An Intercession Accomplished by Christ)

"**P**erfect" is the word chosen by the writer of Hebrews to describe Jesus, our priest. Do you agree? If Christ is the perfect Saviour, having offered the perfect sacrifice and having revealed the Father perfectly, that says something.

Does the temple in Jerusalem need to be rebuilt and animal sacrifice be re-instituted? Not if Jesus was a perfect sacrifice. His death on the cross for all was totally adequate.

Is there a need for some latter-day revelation to show us the way of salvation? After Jesus, others like Mohammed or Joseph Smith have arisen claiming to be God's prophets. Yet, if Jesus of Nazareth was not only the perfect sacrifice for sins but the perfect revelation, then God's will has been fully made known to man. No inadequacies need supplementation. No inaccuracies need correction.

Review the argument of the epistle to the Hebrews. In chapters 1 and 2 Jesus is presented as the perfect revelation. He is more than the prophets who spoke to Israel and greater than the angels who brought the law to Sinai. In chapters 3 and 4 Christ is shown to be the perfect deliverer, greater than both Moses and Joshua. Now in chapters 5, 6 and 7 the Lord is heralded as the perfect priest. There had been many priests. There also had been in each generation high priests. But, Jesus is the highest priest of all. He is totally different. In what way? Let an acrostic on the word "priest" remind you of six ways Jesus is different from all the priests before him.

DIFFERENT IN HIS PERSON

Allow the "P" in the word priest to remind you of Christ's person. Jesus is a unique person. He is special. He is not like those from Levi. Jesus was from the tribe of Judah. All other Jewish priests were married. They had of necessity to be, for the priesthood was an hereditary office. They were mortal men and their work had to be passed on at their death to others. But this Jesus, God's "Son" (5:5) was "a priest forever" (5:6). He is able to offer us "eternal salvation" (5:9) because he ever lives as the overcomer of death. Hence, he need not marry and bear physical offspring who will carry on an unfinished work. He is a priest of a higher order, whose ministry on man's behalf will go on without end.

In Old Testament story, if a man was a priest, he likely was just a priest and not a prophet. Were he a prophet, his ministry usually neither included that of priest nor king. Jesus again is different. He is all in all. He is prophet and priest and king. John 3:16 calls Jesus God's "only begotten Son." μονογενής means unique. Jesus is the only one of his kind. Others may be called children of God by adoption. They are never sons of God in the same sense as Jesus. He is unique in his person. "And in none other is there salvation: for neither is there any other name under heaven, that is given among men, wherein we must be saved" (Acts 4:12).

There may be many teachers. There is only one Saviour. There may be many Buddhas. Gautama was only one of the "enlightened ones." Jesus is the only Son of God. The apostle John wrote of the "many antichrists" that had risen. There may be a plurality of antichrists. There ever will be but one true Christ.

Peter made the good confession at Caesarea Philippi saying that Jesus was "the Christ, the Son of the living God" (Matt. 16:16). He did not call this teacher a Christ, or a Son. He affirmed Jesus to be "the Christ, the Son." But read ahead in Matthew's next chapter, where the transfiguration is being witnessed. Moses (representing the Law) and Elijah (representing the Prophets) are there with Jesus. Jesus' face and garments are shining as the sun. Peter offers to make three tabernacles, one for each of the three persons. His suggestion considers the trio as if they were equals. God the Father points out the clear distinction. He sends a cloud to overshadow them. His voice rings out the clear declaration, "This is my beloved Son . . . hear ye him" (Matt. 17:5). In that very moment Moses and Elijah vanish away. Only Jesus remains. He is not to be seen as only another lawgiver like Moses. He is not to be considered but one of a line of prophets like Elijah. Jesus is more. Jesus is different from the many servants that God has inspired for service. Only "in the name of Jesus every knee should bow . . . and . . . every tongue should confess that Jesus Christ is Lord, to the glory of God the Father" (Phil. 2:10-11).

DIFFERENT IN HIS RIGHTEOUSNESS

Of Jesus it could be said, "in all points tempted like as we are, yet without sin" (Heb. 4:15). God intended for all priests to be righteous. But, every one fell short. God meant that His high priests, especially, should be holy men. In the earthly days of Christ, the high priests were Annas and Caiaphas. Guilty men they were, clamoring for both the death of Jesus and that of those who proclaimed him. They wore robes that marked them as holy, but in their hearts was iniquity.

How otherwise was the Master! Jesus committed no sin. No guile was found in his mouth. He was "holy, guileless, undefiled, separated from sinners, and made higher than the heavens" (Heb. 7:26). We look at Congressmen, Senators and civic leaders, respecting them as the community's finest examples. Trusting their character, we placed them in high office. Then the newspaper makes headlines with some scandal in high places. Among men, there ever will be disappointing weaknesses. According to the mystery religions of pagan Rome and Greece such frailty existed among the gods. Their deities were made in the image of men. They were guilty of incest, murder and every vice.

A PRIEST THAT IS DIFFERENT

The priests of Israel might be garbed in glorious array. The white garment might speak of a righteousness unattained by the priest himself. Jesus was different. He was different in person and he was different in righteousness.

DIFFERENT IN HIS INTERCESSION

If Jesus were only unique in holiness but not in love, there would be no gospel. Hear this truth: Jesus hates sin but Jesus loves sinners. If he only detested iniquity, we would live in fear of him. He would come down upon us in wrath. If he only loved sinners and did not hate sin, he would wink at our evil and pass it by. The real Jesus of Scripture is holy and righteous. He is loving. He also is sinless. He is both "just, and the justifier of him that hath faith in Jesus" (Rom. 3:26).

What an intercessor is Christ! "In all points tempted," but in no point sinning. He is the "one mediator also between God and men, himself man, Christ Jesus" (I Tim. 2:5). How we need such a person to represent us before God, since we have all fallen short of his glory. We need an advocate who hasn't sinned, but we must have one who we know has felt temptation's tug. If Jesus were only loving, he might be too tolerant of sin. Were he only righteous he might be too harsh and condemning of our weakness. Christ makes the perfect priest, for, though never sinning, he is known always to be sympathetic.

A priest was called "to offer both gifts and sacrifices for sins . . . as for the people, so also for himself to offer for sins" (Heb. 5:1-3). Our Saviour, having no sins of his own, makes a much better intercessor. We need not go through Mary, angels or saints to God. The one "Advocate with the Father" is "Jesus Christ the righteous: and he is the propitiation for our sins" (I John 2:1-2). Because he has known temptation, we know he understands. We recognize that he "can bear gently with the ignorant and erring" (Heb. 5:2). God always has understood. Yet man could not grasp so grand a truth, when in his weakness he succumbed to the Tempter. Humanity could not accept that He who is Spirit could be sympathetic to men in the flesh. Then came the incarnation and Jesus took on human form. He in the flesh faced trial "with strong crying and tears" (Heb. 5:7) and emerged victor. We need such an intercessor.

Luke 15:1-2 tells of "publicans and sinners . . . drawing near" to listen to Jesus. They felt comfortable in his presence. Never once did he lower himself to share in their sins. Rather always he helped them get right with God. He is a merciful and gentle intermediary. Always he was holy. Ever he was helpful. They did not yet know the song of C.F. Weigle, but they all recognized the truth, "No One Ever Cared for Me Like Jesus."[1] He detests sins. He loves sinners. He offers freedom this very hour.

THE DIFFERENT IN HIS EFFICACY

"P" in the word priest, reminds us that Jesus is different in his person from all who preceded and followed him. "R" speaks of Christ's righteousness that had no flaws. "I" brings to mind the Master's intercession that has no equal. The "E" stands for his efficacy which is perfect. Efficacy is a big word. It inquires what effect a thing has. It asks if the purpose of an act is accomplished.

The Old Testament tells of sheep and oxen being sacrificed in the temple. Was it efficacious? Were the sins of the people taken away? The Bible answer is, "It is impossible that the blood of bulls should take away sins" (Heb. 10:4). Animal offerings might suggest that one day there would be provided "the Lamb of God that taketh away the sin of the world" (John 1:29). Until that day, the sacrifices at the altar only reminded men that sin brought death and that the Lord one day would provide a vicarious substitute in His Messiah. Now that Jesus had come, had defeated the Devil at every turn and had suffered the death of the cross, he was "made perfect . . . the author of eternal salvation" (Heb. 5:8-9).

Since that great day, when Jesus "died for our sins according to the scriptures" (I Cor. 15:3), we have promise of "the remission of sins" (Acts 2:38). Believers know that "sins may be blotted out" (Acts 3:19). They rejoice that there is "now no condemnation" (Rom. 8:2).

On the day of atonement (*Yom Kippur*), the high priest of old passed beyond the temple's veil with the blood that had been offered on the altar of sacrifice. His intention was to deal with the sin problem. In fact, however, no sin was taken away. Rather the guilt of the last year was but rolled ahead to be handled later. No sin was cancelled or marked "paid in full." In Israel this practice was carried out year after year, yet the problem of sin was still there. The high priest's application of animal blood was comparable to making an interest payment on a back-breaking debt, but the debt itself was remaining unpaid. Then Jesus came as both God's high priest and as God's lamb. He took the law of sin and death. He nailed it to the cross. On the A.D. side of the event of Calvary, all the blood-washed saints can sing:

> You ask me why I'm happy? So I'll just tell you why. Its because my sins are gone. And when I meet the scoffers who ask me where they are, I say, my sins are gone. They are underneath the blood of the cross of Calvary, as far removed as darkness is from dawn. In the sea of God's forgetfulness, that's good enough for me. Praise God, my sins are gone.[2]

Those sins were many. They were heavy. Yet Jesus took them on himself, and became sin for us. Today, in the eyes of God, we stand spotless before His throne.

The adequacy and excellence of Christ's sacrifice is a major point in the Epistle to the Hebrews. The recipients of the letter are under temptation to go back to Judaism. In that religion, at that time, Jews did have at their temple a sacrifice for sins. But such a sacrifice, should it contain the blood of thousands of animals, could not remove one sin (cp. Heb. 10:4). The better sacrifice God provided in Christ is "perfect" in bringing "eternal salvation" (5:9).

The sacrificial lamb in Israel had to be spotless and without blemish. It must be a male. In the Christian system the figures mix. No Old Testament priest could offer himself as the lamb. Yet Jesus our High Priest is also "the Lamb of God, that taketh away the sin of the world!" (John 1:29). Hear the New Testament reminders of Christ's self-giving. Ephesians 5:26 reads, "Christ also loved the church and gave himself up for it." Mark 10:45 says, "the Son of man also came not to be ministered unto, but to minister, and to give his life a ransom for many."

Never before was there a sacrifice like that. Paul refers to it as a divine sacrifice. Hear him address the Ephesian elders, "Take heed unto yourselves, and to all the flock. . . . Feed the church of the Lord which he purchased with his own blood" (Acts 20:28). The King James Version, along with the two oldest Greek manuscripst, calls it "the church of God" purchased by His own blood. The price of our redemption was not the blood of an animal. It was more than the blood of a mere mortal. Required was the blood of God-incarnate to handle the sin problem.

DIFFERENT IN HIS TITLE

What title was given this unique person — unique in righteousness, intercession and efficacy? By what term did the saved refer to this one who offered himself as the perfect sacrifice? He was "named of God a high priest after the order of Melchizedek" (Heb. 5:10).

Take a short course in the Hebrew language, for every recipient of the Epistle to the Hebrews knew the meaning of that name Melchizedek. The first half of the title is the word meaning king. The second half means righteousness. Thus Jewish ears at the reference to Melchizedek heard "king of righteousness." This Old

Testament man was "king of Salem" (Gen. 14:18), possibly the later Jerusalem. The eastern greeting of *shalom*, or peace, carries the concept. This ancient character is held up in Hebrews 7 as a type of Jesus, the king of righteousness and peace.

Our hearts sing, "King of my life I crown Thee now, Thine shall the glory be."[3] We see the cross, emblem of torture, transformed into a throne. No longer is the dreadful rood a symbol of judgment. It has become a reminder of grace.

To sing and talk about our king-priest is not alone sufficient. The benefits of the sacrifice made by our priest must be applied personally to each of us. Jesus' "obedience" (Heb. 5:8) was essential to our salvation. He became "obedient even unto the death, yea, the death of the cross" (Phil. 2:8). Who then shall be forgiven? Which ones of this fallen race shall know "eternal salvation"? The clear Bible answer is, "all them that obey him" (Heb. 5:9). I know you believe the gospel, but have you obeyed its terms? The New Testament promises eventual condemnation "to them that obey not the gospel of our Lord Jesus" (II Thess. 1:8). Believe the facts. Obey the commands. Enjoy the promises.

Endnotes

    1. *Christian Service Songs* (Winona Lake, IN: The Rhodeheaver Hall Mack Co., 1939), p. 57.
    2. N.B. Vandall, "My Sins Are Gone," *New Songs of Inspiration* (Nashville: John T. Benson Co., n.d.), p. 12.
    3. Jennie E. Hussey, "Lead Me to Calvary," *Favorite Hymns of Praise* (Wheaton, IL: Tabernacle Publishing Co., 1976), p. 337.

CHAPTER NINE

You Ought to Be Teachers
Hebrews 5:11-6:3

(An Intercession Taught by the Church)

Are you glad to be a part of a Bible-believing, Bible-teaching church? Before you answer, think a moment. All Christians enjoy hearing what Jesus has done on their behalf. It is a time of elation when we celebrate the incarnation, the crucifixion story and the resurrection victory. It is a happy experience to hear again the hope of Jesus' return and our ascension to be with him forever. No person fails to appreciate reminders of what the Lord has done for him or her. But are you and I equally uplifted in hearing God's expectations of us? What God expects of His people is included in the teaching of the churches that proclaim the entire counsel of God.

The first readers of Hebrews saw the words addressed to them: "by reason of the time, ye ought to be teachers" (5:12). The inspired writer was telling them that they ought to be something they were not. The "what-ought-to-be" was one thing. The "what-was" fell far short. God's high expectations were not being met. The ones who had been receiving the gospel for a period of time were content to remain receivers. Heaven's plan was that receivers develop into sharers. The recipient of yesterday was expected to be the teacher of today.

Before we compare our present situation with theirs, let's do a little arithmetic. The people being addressed in the epistle are possibly Jewish converts to Christ that Paul had won during his Roman imprisonment that began A.D. 61. If we are right in dating the book of Hebrews at A.D. 68, these people had been followers of Christ for seven years.

How long have you been a disciple of Jesus? Have you lived up to God's dream and desire for you, that by this "time ye ought to be teachers" (5:12)? Are you content to remain a listener? Have I become "dull of hearing" (5:11)? Do you "have need again that some one teach you the rudiments of the first principles" (5:12)? Are both of us still babes needing "milk and not solid food?"

To anyone who has been a follower of Jesus at least seven years, learn that it is time you became teachers. Let all who love Bible teaching hear the lesson of our text. It is time to get enrolled (6:1-2). It is time to get enriched (5:13-14). It is time to get involved (5:11-12).

IT IS TIME TO GET ENROLLED

We all start with the "A B C's." We begin with "the first principles of the oracles of God" (Heb. 5:12). These rudiments of the faith are given in Hebrews 6:1-2. They are called "the doctrine of the first principles of Christ." They are referred to as the "foundation."

The six items listed are the kind of topics preached where ever missionaries or evangelists go to start a church. Four of the things listed refer to items at either the commencement of a Christian life or the establishment of a Christian congregation. The final two items are the ultimate happenings at the end of time.

"Repentance . . . faith . . . the teaching of baptism" are human responses to the proclaimed gospel. Each case of conversion recorded in Acts makes familiar these terms. Let us do some defining.

"Repentance" is a part of the enrollment process in the church. μετανοέω is the Greek word for repent. It is from the words νοῦς, meaning mind and μετά referring to a change. It means to change one's mind in such a way that one's conduct is transformed. The Jewish readers are reminded that their repentance was "from dead works." That is, their earlier attempts to live up to God's commandments had fallen short. Those efforts at righteousness were impotent to bring them salvation. Such works were dead as far as accomplishing forgiveness. God's work for them at the cross was full of life-giving power. Human effort cannot avail. Let all men turn from putting faith in their own dead works. Let them turn in trust to God's acts for them in Christ.

"Faith" that saves is not self-confidence and reliance upon personal achievements. It is rather "faith toward God." Someone made an acrostic on the word faith: "**F**orsaking **A**ll **I T**ake **H**im." That is what faith is. It is not just the mental assent to a creedal statement, like "there is a God and Jesus is His Son." It is also the placing of one's total trust in him as one's personal Lord and Saviour.

"Baptism" comes next for the penitent believer, as he enrolls in God's church. Hebrews 6:2 uses the plural "baptisms." John the Baptist practiced a baptism that foreshadowed the coming Messiah's saving work. Jesus called his death and overwhelming suffering the baptism he awaited. After his resurrection and before his ascension, he commissioned the church to baptize those that accepted the preaching of his gospel. As John's water baptism looked forward to the passion and resurrection of God's Messiah, the church's water and Spirit baptism looks back to those saving events.

For centuries people have come to Christ through faith, repentance and baptism and have received the welcome of warm "hands" reaching out to accept them (cp. Gal. 2:9). By the "laying on of hands" some members were set aside to serve as deacons, or elders, or in other service capacities (cp. Acts 6:1-6; 13:2-3). By the "laying on of hands," apostles were used of the Holy Spirit to give a variety of miraculous powers to first century servants (cp. II Tim. 1:6).

At the end of each of the synoptic Gospels is recorded Jesus' great commission to his followers. Matthew's account speaks of "baptizing" (28:19). Mark's record calls for faith, or believing, along with that baptism (16:16). Luke's words include the call for "repentance" (24:47). Faith, repentance and baptism are not only in the orders of Jesus, according to the written Gospels, they are also in the accounts of apostolic practice. The book of Acts shows the church obedient to Christ's orders.

The first gospel sermon in Acts called for faith in Jesus as Lord and Christ. This was followed by the call to repentance and baptism (Acts 2:36-38). Was Saul's conversion an exception? Faith was there. He was called upon to "arise and be baptized" (Acts 22:16). But where was the repentance? Does not three days of prayer indicate that even when the word is not used the act is evident? Was the Philippian Jailor's conversion in this pattern? He was called upon to "Believe on the Lord Jesus" (Acts 16:31). He was "baptized" (16:33). Again the word repentance is omitted, but not the act. Read of the washing of the prisoner's stripes. Faith in Christ, repentance toward Christ and baptism into Christ are a part of the A B C's of the Gospel. Yet even to this hour some are D.E.F. (deaf) to the offer.

Should one wonder why along with the announcement of the steps of salvation there is the reference to "resurrection . . . and . . . eternal judgment"? I believe it is to encourage the right choice. There will be eternal consequences. Each man will be saved or lost — in Christ or out of Christ. In this world a person is free to go from one side to the other. Today the doors of the church are open wide. Conversion is possible. But after death has come, judgment comes. According to Jesus, "a great gulf fixed" after death makes impossible the passing from hell to heaven or Abraham's bosom to hades (cp. Luke 16:19-31).

You and I, Dives and Lazarus can do some changing in this life. But after our earthly life is over there is eternal judgment and it is departure from Christ into "eternal fire" (Matt. 24:41).

Choose whom ye will serve. Faith, repentance, baptism and the welcoming hand bring you in. These steps prepare you for the resurrection and the judgment. If you already are enrolled, what is the next step?

IT IS TIME TO GET ENRICHED

To enter the church is to be enrolled in Christ's school. In that body are those who will tutor you as disciples. They will attempt to help you grow.

A student signing up for a college course will want to know the textbook that the professor will use. The first thing he will do upon enrollment will be to buy the text to be studied. Christians will need to acquire the library of sixty-six books we call the Bible.

The Psalmist David exalted God's word. He saw it as the source of an enriched life. Psalm 119 is a song containing 176 verses. Each line extols Jehovah's revelation. The first eight sentences about God's law start with a Hebrew *aleph*. Then there are eight that begin with Hebrew *beth*. This continues by eights until each letter of the Hebrew alphabet has been marshalled in a paean of praise to the law of the Lord. You read such an inquiry as "Wherewithal shall a young man cleanse his way?" You hear the answer, "By taking heed thereto according to thy word" (119:9).

In the earlier Psalm 19 you read of three preachers that make God known. "The heavens declare the glory of God" (19:1). Nature is not silent. It proclaims the Creator. Toward the end of the Psalm, David says one's life gives testimony. He pleads, "Let the words of my mouth and the meditation of my heart be acceptable in thy sight" (19:4). Between the preaching of nature and the proclamation of our lives, the testimony of Jehovah's law is called "perfect, restoring the soul" (19:7).

A follower of Jesus ought to own the Biblical library of law, prophets, psalms, gospels, epistles and apocalypse. He ought also learn how to divide it correctly and how to use it rightly.

Martin Luther had a good suggestion. He said that when you pick apples you shake the tree and pick up the fruit that fell. Next you shake a major limb and gather some more apples. When that is done you move to the smaller branches. Treat the Bible the same. Gather the thought of a major chapter. Go over it again a verse at a time. Further truths can be gleaned as you then turn to single words.

Alexander Campbell, a significant leader of the Reformation of the nineteenth century, was troubled by "textuary preachers." These might deal with but a single verse in their Sunday morning homilies. Should their congregations be in attendance all fifty-two Sundays of the year, they would need to live as long as Methuselah to get a Bible education. Expository sermons that deal with larger portions of Scripture or those that have scope were to be preferred. A listener who gleaned from tree to major limbs to smaller branches, would soon be equipped to teach others.

Let him who is once enrolled, begin to get enriched. Buy the library of sixty-six books, called the Bible. Study your text. Do your assignments. To be in the school and own the text is not sufficient. Each pupil must do the work required.

IT IS TIME TO GET INVOLVED

Have you noticed that we are working backward

through the Hebrews' text? Hebrews 6:1-2 implied that at first each person is to get enrolled. Hebrews 5:13-14 called on all who had started to get enriched, becoming "full grown men." The earlier verse 12 observed that it was now time for getting involved. "By reason of the time ye ought to be teachers."

You may call to your defense Ephesians 4:11: "And he gave some to be . . . teachers." I may quote I Corinthians 12:28, "And God hath set some in the church . . . teachers." These texts are correct. There is a sense in which all of us are not to be set aside for the special ministry of teaching. God would not have all his body be a mouth and publicly instruct the gathered church. But there are other ways to teach and preach without doing it in a professional manner in the specialized sense. Timothy was set aside to "do the work of an evangelist" (II Tim. 4:5), but all the saved were to be soul-winners.

The word "kindergarten" suggests children (*kinder*) are like flowers lovingly grown in the garden (*garten*). In every church its small tots are nurtured in the way of the Lord. Across the years you see developing tomorrow's missionaries, teachers and congregational stalwarts. Every Christian home ought to be a school. Each father and mother ought to be a teacher of the tender lives entrusted to his and her care. By this time all of us should be in some real sense instructors. The tutoring can be done in various ways and in a variety of places.

Who should teach? Every follower of the Master Teacher. Where should the instruction take place? We will only be limited by short-sighted imaginations. When should the sharing of truth occur? Acts 5:41 tells of first century disciples in these words: "And every day, in the temple and at home, they ceased not to teach and to preach Jesus as the Christ." We of this later century may not do our teaching and sharing of the gospel in a temple setting, but we ought to be communicating our faith in our homes, in our classrooms and in our communities. Find a way suitable to you. But be teachers!

How can we get involved in this teaching? Simply realize that God has blessed us in order that we can bless others. First the acorn, then the oak tree. First the egg, then the chicken. First the learner, then the teacher. In all cases growth ought to come. In your case be a preacher and a reacher. Let each teach. Frank Laubach advocated, "Each one teach one." In no other way can the world be won. There will never be enough professional preachers to evangelize the world. But right now, if each one would but reach one, the globe would soon be covered with the gospel "as the waters cover the sea" (Isa. 11:9).

I foresee a great future for every congregation where its people get enrolled. I prophesy victory for each body of believers that week-by-week gathers to get enriched. I predict numerical and spiritual growth for each unit of the kingdom of Christ when its members get involved in the struggle for the minds and souls of men.

CHAPTER TEN

Red Flares and Vanishing Clouds
Hebrews 6:4-20

(An Intercession Forfeited by the Foolish)

Red flares are set out where an accident has occurred. Their purpose is to warn drivers to avoid the dangers ahead. Each traveler coming upon the scene is cautioned to slow down and to take exceptional care to avoid getting involved in a harmful or fatal tragedy.

We meet such a flare in Hebrews 6:4-20. The dreadful and real danger of apostasy from Christ is held before the readers. In Paul's epistles he generally deals with doctrine in the first portion of his writings and turns to life application toward the end. Our author not only will reserve his last three chapters for practical appeals, he will insert several times along the way in earlier parts of his work warnings, pleas and calls for action. He anticipates safe travel all the way to glory for his readers, as he writes, "But, beloved, we are persuaded better things of you, and things that accompany salvation, though we thus speak" (6:9). That is, the stormy clouds really are there. They need to be recognized for the dangers they forebode, but by God's help and the readers' responsiveness, the black sky will not remain in their case. The clouds will vanish and blue skies will return. Yet, let all the forgiven learn three things about salvation. You can find it. You can lose it. Or, you can keep it.

Let us use Hebrews 6:9 as a tool for digging out the truths about the wonder of salvation, the real possibility of apostasy and the better probability of perseverance to the end. Note the phrase regarding "things that accompany salvation." Can we discover from our text what accompanies salvation, what accompanies apostasy and what accompanies steadfastness? If our eyes are open we not only can, but we will.

YOU CAN FIND IT

Several years ago many cars were being driven that had bumper stickers with the three words, "I Found It." A nation-wide campaign for Christian converts used the phrase in their advertising. The life-changing discovery referred to was salvation through Christ. The author of Hebrews lists several blessings from God that become ours when we find Christ, or better expressed, when Jesus finds us.

The believers were said to be "once enlightened" (6:4). That is, they had heard the informative gospel. The church in Ephesus you recall, was informed, "Ye were once darkness, but are now light in the Lord" (Eph. 5:8). It was Jesus' desire and command that "all the world" should hear the preaching of this good-news (Mark

16:15) in order that "the light of the gospel of the glory of Christ" (II Cor. 4:4) should dispel all darkness.

Every individual that is "in Christ," first has heard what God has done for him and how he ought now to respond to receive his salvation. Tied to the historic facts of Jesus' ministry are the glorious promises of our redemption. Those "enlightened" by the church's proclamation of Christ crucified and risen have "tasted of the heavenly gift." The question "what gift?" is answered by Paul's words, "For the wages of sin is death; but the free gift of God is eternal life in Christ Jesus our Lord" (Rom. 6:23). Jesus taught the same in the "God so loved the world" passage that promises believers "eternal life" (John 3:16). Another way to define the gift we have tasted is to use the synonym, salvation. "For by grace have ye been saved through faith . . . it is the gift of God" (Eph. 2:8).

To be sure of the meaning of the phrase, "tasted of the heavenly gift," compare chapter 2:9 of the same book, Hebrews. Christ did "taste of death for every man." Jesus did not just appear to die, he died. The Lord did not only seem to experience death, he actually was dead. The persons being described by the writer of Hebrews did not only look like Christians, they were Christians. To "taste of death" in Biblical parlance means to die (cp. Matt. 16:28; John 8:52). To have "tasted of the heavenly gift" means to have received salvation and life.

Christians are ones who have been enlightened by the gospel, have experienced heaven's gift and have been "made partakers of the Holy Spirit." Without the indwelling of the Spirit of Christ, no person today can be said to belong to Christ (cp. Rom. 8:9). Before Jesus ascended on high, having experienced Calvary and resurrection, "the Spirit was not yet given; because Jesus was not yet glorified" (John 7:39). But ever since Christ's ascension and coronation, believers upon their repentance and baptism "receive the gift of the Holy Spirit." That is heaven's promise to "all that . . . God shall call unto him" (Acts 2:38-39).

Those who "were made partakers of the Holy Spirit" were said also to have "tasted the good word of God." When you take God's book that is crammed with promises and you consume it, like John the Revelator did the little book given him in Revelation 10:9, you will sing about God's word, with David, "More to be desired are they then gold, yea, than much fine gold; Sweeter also than honey and the droppings of the honeycomb" (Psa. 19:10).

Taste the promise, "And my God shall supply every need of yours according to his riches in glory in Christ Jesus" (Phil. 4:19).Or revel in the hopeful word, "the peace of God, which passeth all understanding, shall guard your hearts and your thoughts in Christ Jesus" (Phil. 4:7). Experience the message of assurance, "all things work together for good, even to them that are called according to his purpose" (Rom. 8:28).

No promise from God ever fails. One man's Bible was marked page after page with the letters T and P in the margins. One could note that often the two letters were written by a different pen or pencil than the other. It was explained that the Bible student, upon coming to a promise in his reading of Scripture, would write a T at the verse. This meant he would TRY it. After God proved Himself faithful to that promise, the Christian wrote in the P for PROVEN.

The red-flares of warning in Hebrews 6 are to catch the attention of believers who not only have feasted on God's faithful promises. They even have experienced "the powers of the age to come." They have shared in blessings and joys that give foretaste of the eternal world. The very gospel, at every hearing, proved to be "the power of God unto salvation" (Rom. 1:16).

YOU CAN LOSE IT

A reading of Hebrews 6:4-5 describes a redeemed man. The items listed are among the "things that accompany salvation" (6:9). Were the extra-Biblical slogan "Once saved, always saved" a rule without possible exception, the red flares of warning would not concern us. Regarding God's salvation it can be said from Hebrews 6:4-5, "You can find it." The next lines in Hebrews 6:6-8 warn "You can lose it." As we have listed some things that accompany salvation, let us search for that which accompanies apostasy.

We early in our study met the word "neglect." The question was raised, "how shall we escape, if we neglect so great a salvation?" (Heb. 2:3) We later learn that some believers under external pressure were "forsaking . . . assembling together" (10:25). It is obvious to all that a hot ember, lifted by tongs from the burning wood of a fireplace and set by itself, gradually but certainly will grow cold. It should have been clear to believers that neglect of one's spiritual life and isolation from activities of the church body posed a real danger. We need each other. The Christian religion is personal but it is never private. Each person who is joined to Christ the Head is, of necessity, attached to the body which is the church. Christ-likeness is not just a word. It has meaning. Jesus did not hold himself aloof from the religious community where he lived. Of our example it is written, "he entered, as his custom was, into the synagogue on the sabbath day" (Luke 4:16). What accompanies the loss of salvation? Negligence is one characteristic of the soul in peril of possible apostasy.

Another warning sign is spiritual dullness. Hebrews sounds the alarm, "Ye are become dull of hearing" (5:11). How different were the Bereans that Luke termed "noble." These men and women "received the word with all readiness of mind, examining the scriptures daily" (Acts 17:11). How basic it is for each of God's people to hear Paul's advice: "Give diligence to present thyself approved unto God, a workman that needeth not to be ashamed, handling aright the word of truth" (II Tim. 2:15). In some modern Sunday Schools, a Bible-study group will select the name, the FBI class. They are wishing to be Faithful Bible Investigators. Probing the Scriptures on a regular basis is apostolic and not apostate. The road to spiritual destruction is paved with negligence regarding the assembly and dullness regarding the word.

The sirens of heaven sound warning when a churchman, even for a moment, toys with the idea of breaking away from Christianity. Acceptance of Christ brings the joy of salvation. Rejection of Christ brings the gloom of damnation. The circumstance facing the Jewish Christians receiving the letter we call Hebrews was this. Many believers under Nero were facing death and suffering for no other crime than wearing the name "Christian" (cp. I Pet. 4:16). These Hebrews thus far were spared in that they were being considered more as Jews than as followers of Christ. They had "not yet resisted unto blood" (Heb. 12:4). Would they, to save their necks, "crucify to themselves the Son of God afresh, and put him to an open shame" (Heb. 6:6)?

We are not here discussing backsliding but willful apostasy. There is a difference between a disciple that "fell" under a temptation and one that "fell away." The former can find forgiveness upon repentance. Concerning the latter it is written, "It is impossible to renew them again unto repentance" (6:6). The congregation is well advised that seeks diligently to restore any in the flock whose membership in the body becomes inactive. The end of such a careless road of negligence and dullness could be willful rejection.

Unproductivity is an additional item to be on the watch for among the "things that accompany" apostasy rather than "salvation" (6:9). Hebrews 6:7 parallels a fruitful life lived for God and "land . . . that bringeth forth herbs." The next verse describes an unproductive life that "beareth thorns and thistles." Such a soul "is rejected and nigh unto a curse; whose end is to be burned" (6:8). Jesus had taught the same when he said, "Every branch in me that beareth not fruit, he taketh it away" (John 15:2).

Examine your life as I examine mine. Do I find the items listed in Hebrews 6:4-5 that accompany salvation?

Do I note any danger signs that accompany apostasy? Cancer is curable if detected early. Ultimate and final apostasy can be stopped, if we heed the Great Physician's words to watch for symptoms like those described in Hebrews 6:6-8. Are you getting "sluggish" (Heb. 6:12)? Anyone who one time has mired down in the mud with his vehicle knows the need to keep momentum. Any believer is safer when his life keeps progressing spiritually. Get sluggish and you could become stopped for good.

YOU CAN KEEP IT

Our author is a realist and he is an optimist. He knows it is possible for a man to find salvation and lose it. The red flares in the passage are true warning concerning a real danger. However, he also knows it is possible for a man to find salvation and to keep it. This he expects from his readers.

"But, beloved we are persuaded better things of you, and things that accompany salvation, though we thus speak" (Heb. 6:9). A scan reading of the rest of the chapter reveals qualities that accompany steadfastness.

He first names ministry. "God is not unrighteous to forget your work and the love which ye showed toward his name, in that ye ministered unto the saints (in Rome), and still do minister" (6:10). Every Christian at his baptism is ordained to the ministry of Christ. God's enablers, such as "pastors and teachers" are "for the perfecting of the saints, unto the work of ministering" (Eph. 4:11-12).

The conjunction "and" adds to their "work" also "the love . . . showed toward his name." Who needs this evidence of steadfastness from you? Who hungers for a loving touch? Children need to be loved. Married partners are lifted by hearing the words "I love you" repeated for the umteenth time. The elderly glow when they sense that you really care. Missionaries and preachers, like all other human beings, blossom at words of appreciation. What sunshine and showers do for the garden, your expressions of love do for all that you meet.

Those lives in Christ that evidence they are destined for glory, show ministry, love, faith and patience. Those that "inherit the promises" are said to have both of these last two qualities of "faith and patience" (6:12). Faith is trust. Patience is faithfulness or endurance. Hope concludes the list and is called "an anchor of the soul, a hope both sure and steadfast and entering into that which is within the veil" (6:18).

Seamen cast their anchors down into the blue sea. Christians cast their anchor of hope upward beyond the blue sky. The veil of the temple hid from view the cubical "holy of holies" that typified heaven. Jesus, as our High Priest, is the One in whom his followers anchor for security. They confidently sing,

> We have an anchor that keeps the soul
> Steadfast and sure while the billows roll.
> Fastened to the Rock which cannot move,
> Grounded firm and deep in the Saviour's love.[1]

When I am asked if I believe in the doctrine of eternal security, I often reply that I certainly do not believe in the doctrine of infernal insecurity. I find the Bible in all its parts, and certainly in Hebrews 6, to show the possibility of apostasy. The red flares of warning are real. Yet, with the author of Hebrews, I predict vanishing clouds and brighter days for the readers of Christian literature. "Beloved, we are persuaded better things of you, and things that accompany salvation" (6:9). You made it to first base with a single. Or, possibly you are on third. It is possible that even with bases loaded, no score will be registered. The runner must get all the way home. This chapter of our study carefully outlines dangers that could count you out. But it also optimistically encourages traits that will bring you safely all the way home.

Endnotes

1. Priscilla J. Owens, "We Have an Anchor," *The New Church Hymnal* (Waco, TX: Lexicon Music, Inc., 1976), p. 46.

CHAPTER ELEVEN

Meet Your King
Hebrews 7:1-28

(An Intercession Exemplified by Melchizedek)

The superiority of Christ is the theme of Hebrews. Jesus is said to be "better" than the prophets and angels in message, more successful in deliverance than Moses and Joshua, and more helpful in ministry than all the priests of Jewish history. At the center and core of the epistle, chapter 7, Jesus is shown to be even greater than Melchizedek.

When the author of Hebrews looked at the pages of his Old Testament, he saw God's Messiah reflected everywhere. Jesus and his church were mirrored in the people, places and things told of in the first Bible book to the last. The ancient events typified Christian history. The personalities were examples of some aspect to Jesus' ministry. The gospel was foreshadowed in building and furniture, rivers and floods, manna and oil. When the author read of sacrificial lambs, he visualized Jesus. When he saw incense, lavers or candelabra, he pictured prayer, baptism and divine revelation.

Paging through Genesis to what we label chapter 14, the author of Hebrews found eternal significance in the passing relationship between Abraham and this special priest concerning which little was known. The poetic lines that you have often heard proved true again. The relationship between Old and New Covenants is supplemental. "The old is in the new explained. The new was in the old contained. The old is in the new revealed. The new was in the old concealed."[1] Christians today, like Abraham of old, walk by faith. Jesus in this age, like Melchizedek in patriarchal times, offers blessings to those who receive him as "priest of God Most High" (Gen. 14:18).

From the well of Hebrews 7 let us draw out six waterpots of refreshing spiritual drink for our instruction in the Christian faith.

JESUS IS PRINCE OF PEACE

The first parallel our author notes between Melchizedek and Christ has to do with peace. Jerusalem means "city of peace." Melchizedek, the priest-king ruled from Salem (cp. Psa. 76:2). The place of reign may be disputed but not its typology. Clearly this "King of Salem" speaks of the reality that Jesus is "King of peace" (Heb. 7:2).

Had not the eighth century prophet Isaiah spoken in such terms of the coming one? This Old Testament evangelist announced: "For unto us a child is born, unto us a son is given; and the government shall be upon his shoulder: and his name shall be called Wonderful, Counsellor, Mighty God, Everlasting Father, Prince of Peace" (9:6). The same prophet calls the peace that this promised one will bring as a "perfect peace." He declared, "Thou wilt keep him in perfect peace whose mind is stayed on thee; because he trusteth in thee" (6:3).

Paul calls on believers to turn from anxiety, letting rather their "requests be made known unto God." He assures them of "the peace of God, which passeth all understanding" (Phil. 4:6-7). Just two verses after he mentions "the peace of God" as the gift desired, he refers to "the God of peace" (verse 8) as the generous donor of such an unspeakable gift. Wherever the God of peace goes, the peace of God will not be far behind.

E. Stanley Jones, in his book *The Way*, told of a person warring with his God, fighting with his neighbors and disputing with his wife. He termed the man's inner conflicts as a civil war. Yet, once that man met Jesus, the prince of peace, all hostility ceased. Peace remained in his heart, for the Prince of peace had been enthroned there.

Each choir voice sings of "peace, like a river" attending its way. Individually redeemed through Christ, every singer echoes, "It is well, it is well with my soul."[2] Each worshiper's heart says the amen at the reading of the Scripture: "Being therefore justified by faith, we have peace with God through our Lord Jesus Christ" (Rom. 5:1).

New Testament epistles often speak of grace and peace in the same contexts (cp. Rom. 5:1-2). These blessings belong together for it is only by God's grace that man can enjoy inner peace. Jesus had promised this unique kind of peace to his disciples whom he knew would be facing tribulation and likely martyrdom. "Peace I leave with you; my peace I give unto you: not as the world giveth, give I unto you" (John 14:27). The peace existing in the world is fragile. It passes away. The peace given by the Prince of peace abides forever.

One art gallery offered artists an opportunity to be in a contest where paintings could be entered on the year's theme which was "Peace." All types of entries competed for the prize. There were scenes of quiet lakes. There were artistic impressions of gentle sunsets. A different concept on canvas received the award of first place by the judges. The artist had created a storm scene, where in the arm of a tree was a mother bird feeding her nestlings in the midst of the lightening flashes. To the apostles who were told, "In the world ye have tribulation," came the assurance, "but be of good cheer; I have overcome the world" (John 16:33).

JESUS IS PRINCE OF RIGHTEOUSNESS

Melchizedek's city, Salem, reminds of the peace that Jesus brings. Melchizedek's name calls attention to Christ's righteousness. To the ear of a Hebrew, as were both writer and recipients of the epistle being studied, this next parallel was easy to see. Melchizedek was "by interpretation, King of righteousness" (7:2). Let all readers understand that as believers like Abraham walk by faith, Jesus like Melchizedek is a king of righteousness.

Peace and righteousness are wedded together and cannot be separated. Only where there is true righteousness can there be lasting peace. Where there is sin there will be conflict.

Sin is the opposite of righteousness. By experience and by revelation we know what sin is, what it does and what it demands. Sin is the transgression of law. Sin is leaving undone what God has asked us to do. Sin is missing the mark. Sin separates us from God and from each other. Sin either demands death as its earned wage, or sin requires that atonement be made and the rebel against God be forgiven. Christ is the Christian's righteousness. That righteousness is not of man's attainment. It is God's gracious gift to those who place faith in His Son.

JESUS IS PRINCE OF INTERCESSION

"Melchizedek, king of Salem" was "priest of God" (Heb. 7:1). That is, he was an intercessor, or mediator between humans and the Deity. Many in number would be the later descendants of Levi serving in such a ministry. But as Melchizedek was greater than they, Jesus is the greatest intercessor of all. Unlike all predecessors, Jesus overcame all temptation that came his way. As our author earlier asserted, "We have not a high priest that cannot be touched with the feeling of our infirmities: but one that hath been in all points tempted like as we are, yet without sin" (4:15). That being the case, mercy and help are ever available from the Prince of intercessors.

How different was Christ from the Levitical

priesthood! Jesus was from the tribe of Judah, not the tribe of Levi (cp.7:13-14). Being mortals, levitical priests died and were of necessity replaced. Jesus arose from the dead and lives "after the power of an endless life" and is thus "a priest for ever" (7:16-17). Where Jewish priests had "infirmity," our intercessor is God's "Son, perfected for evermore" (7:27).

What an advocate we have! He has invited us to ask, seek and knock at heaven's door. He has encouraged us to make our requests in his name and according to his will. He has welcomed us to come to the throne of grace with the promise, "Hitherto have ye asked nothing in my name: ask, and ye shall receive, that your joy may be made full" (John 16:24).

JESUS IS PRINCE OF A NEW ORDER

The Old Testament contained the New Testament in picture prophecy. The shadow of Melchizedek foretold the substance of Christ, God's priest-king. The starlight of Genesis 14 was preparing for the daylight of Jesus' greater ministry. If the ancient priest that ministered to Abraham brought a peace or a righteousness or intercession, these fade into insignificance when compared to the reality of the Messiah's better ministry.

Our King of righteousness, prince of peace and Priest of intercession has "by so much . . . become the surety of a better covenant" (7:22). Under this new covenant all becomes new. Under this new covenant we wear a new name. We share a new hope. We have promise of "a new heaven and a new earth, wherein dwells righteousness" (II Pet. 3:13).

"Wherefore if any man is in Christ, he is a new creature: the old things are passed away; behold, they are become new" (II Cor. 5:17). Perhaps you remember the day of your baptism. Likely the preacher lowered you beneath the water, reminding you and all those witnessing of the significance of being "baptized into Christ Jesus" and "into his death." As you came up out of that watery grave you possibly heard the minister's voice again quoting Paul, "We were buried therefore with him through baptism into death: that like as Christ was raised from the dead through the glory of the Father, so we also might walk in newness of life" (Rom. 6:3-4). A new birth, a birth of "water and the Spirit," brought entrance into God's new kingdom.

Under the new covenant everything was new. That point will occupy our author in the remaining chapters. In the present chapter he writes, "For the priesthood being changed, there is made of necessity a change also of the law" (7:12). Let all readers turn from the law of Moses to the law of Christ, from the temporal to the eternal, from the "foregoing commandment because of its weakness and unprofitableness" to the "better hope" (7:18-19). Why? Because Christ alone "is able to save to the uttermost them that draw near unto God through him, seeing he ever liveth to make intercession for them" (7:25).

JESUS IS PRINCE OF CELEBRATION

The major point made in the first half of Hebrews 7 is the blessing Abraham received from the priest-king and the tithe he gave to him. During the church age the weekly celebration of gathered worshipers flows between the receiving of Christ's gifts by the believers and the sharing of their gifts with their high priest. Of primary importance is the place and relationship of the two parties. "But without any dispute the less is blessed of the better" (7:7). The receiver of a blessing is less than the one who gives the blessing. The recipient of the tithe is greater than the giver of the tithe. In the type, Melchizedeck is greater than Abraham. Abraham gave the tithe to Melchizedek. Melchizedek gave the blessing to Abraham. In the anti-type, or fulfillment, Jesus is far greater than his disciples. As disciples of Christ we bring our tithes to him, and we receive our blessing from him.

Often in a Sunday worship service the Lord's Supper is shared and the offering is then taken. In the Genesis account, "Melchizedek, king of Salem brought forth bread and wine; and he was priest of God Most High. And he blessed him" (14:18-19). This was followed by the giving of "a tenth of all" to the priest-king. In our case we have received the cup of blessing in remembrance of all the benefits of Calvary. We then gratefully shared our wealth with our High Priest.

It is not our tithes that purchase Christ's blessing. It is in recall of God's blessings through the communion bread and wine that we bring gifts of gratitude to the Saviour. In the words of Hebrews 7, "here men that die receive tithes; but there one, of whom it is witnessed that he liveth" (v. 8).

Many say tithing is Jewish. There is no doubting that Israel was commanded to tithe. A glance at Deuteronomy or Malachi alone would establish that. But history knows of tithing being practiced in Assyria, Babylonia and Egypt as well. Prior to Levites and long before Moses, we have read of Abraham tithing to Melchizedek. Jacob as early as Bethel vowed to God, "of all that thou shalt give me I will surely give the tenth unto thee" (Gen. 28:22). A Christian's love response would never fall below that of those who had received far less.

As we receive a greater blessing from Christ than Abraham gained from Melchizedek, it seems right that we should give to Jesus more than the tenth that Abraham gave to Melchizedek. The early Church, "upon the first day of the week . . . gathered together to break bread" according to Acts 20:7. Those early Christians were also instructed: "upon the first day of the week let each one of you lay by him in store" according to I Corinthians 16:2. In these passages we find bound together God's blessing and our response to that blessing. The flow of Christian worship on the Lord's day is between God's giving and our receiving, and between our responsive giving back to God and his reception to our gifts.

JESUS IS PRINCE OF ETERNITY

Only four Old Testament verses speak of Melchizedek. In addition to the three verses of Genesis, there was the single verse four of Psalm 110, "Thou art a priest for ever after the order of Melchizedek." The author of Hebrews quoted this line in his fifth chapter (5:6) and twice again in his seventh chapter (7:17,21). Christ is unique from all others for he serves for evermore. Unlike Levites he did not inherit his office from predecessors nor transmit it to successors. He is "priest for ever." The sons of Aaron, being but mortal men, died to minister no more. Every generation of Jews had its new set of priests. Melchizedek in a small way pictured Christ's endless ministry. History bears neither a record of his birth nor a statement of his death. As the anti-type is always greater than the type, so Jesus in reality exceeds the shadow of Melchizedek. Jesus had in truth no origin for he is eternal. Melchizedek, as far as historical records were concerned, was "without father, without mother" (7:3). He, too, was "without genealogy" or recorded offspring to follow him and continue his ministry. This further is parallel to Jesus who as "the Son of God" is "a priest continually."

Christ as Lord of eternity is King of all the past, present and future. He is Priest from everlasting to everlasting. He is unique to all others. "It is witnessed that he liveth" (7:9). He "hath been made, not after the law of a carnal commandment, but after the power of an endless life" (v. 16). He is "a priest forever" (vv. 17-21). "He abideth forever" and thus "hath his priesthood unchangeable" (v. 24).

That being true, what conclusion is to be drawn? It is this, "he is able to save to the uttermost" (and we could add, to the guttermost) "them that draw near unto God through him, seeing he ever liveth to make intercession for them" (v. 25). Who would revert from Christianity to Judaism exchanging "a Son, perfected for evermore" for "high priests, having infirmity" (v. 28)?

The Heavenly Father has provided the best in His

Son. He is our peace and our righteousness. He is the one intercessor and mediator between God and man. He has brought in the new and ever-lasting covenant between the God of heaven and all the willing among the nations of earth. He is the center-piece of the church's Lord's Day celebration, giving his blessing and receiving our offerings. He is the only such helper that in our need is ever present — at every time and in every situation. As we often sing, " 'Tis the grandest theme thro' the ages rung; 'Tis the grandest theme for a mortal tongue; 'Tis the grandest theme that the world e'er sung, 'Our God is able to deliver thee.' "[3]

Endnotes

1. Author unknown.
2. Horatio G. Spafford, "It Is Well with My Soul," *Favorite Hymns of Praise* (Wheaton, IL: Tabernacle Publishing Co., 1967), p. 73.
3. William A. Ogden, "He Is Able to Deliver Thee," *Favorite Hymns of Praise*, (Wheaton, IL: Tabernacle Pub. Co., 1967), p. 35.

PART FOUR
Jesus, the Maker of God's Finest Covenant

CHAPTER TWELVE

There Is A Difference
Hebrews 8:1-13

(The Covenant and Its Newness)

There is a difference between law and grace, between the Old Covenant and the New Covenant. "For the law was given through Moses; grace and truth came through Jesus Christ" (John 1:17). The Old Testament and the New Testament are not identical twins. Although from the same Father, they are not twins at all. They are not even look-alikes.

This particular truth needs to be heard in our world where so much confusion abounds. Lay aside your emotions for a few minutes and gird up your minds. Unless this distinction between covenants is grasped, unless workmen are "rightly dividing the word of truth" or "handling aright" its message (cp. II Tim. 2:15), only confusion will result.

You already are conscious that the Bible is divided into the two distinct parts of Old Testament and New Testament. There is also a vast difference between the

Old and New Covenants, the record of which is borne in these Old and New Testament Scriptures. On the night that Jesus observed with his disciples the final Old Covenant Passover feast, he instituted the new feast of the Lord's supper for his coming church. He said of the cup, "This is my blood of the new covenant, which is poured out for many unto remission of sins" (Matt. 26:28).

There is a difference between the covenant that was coming to an end in Christ's death and the one commencing because of his victory over death. It is this difference that Hebrews 8 highlights. Christ's ministry is said to be "more excellent" and his covenant to be "better," in that it is "enacted upon better promises" (v. 6) than that covenant made with Israel. Jeremiah foretold the "new covenant" and predicted it would differ from the earlier one made at Sinai (Jer. 31:31ff. quoted in Heb. 8:8-12). The writer of Hebrews labels the former covenant "aged" and "nigh unto vanishing away" (8:13).

Today some would still try to place the new wine of the gospel into the old wineskins of the past. They would expect the worship days and the ritual forms of the Old Covenant to be those of New Covenant Christians. Since babies of Jewish parents were born Jews then, it is argued that babies of Christian parents ought to be baptized and recognized as Christians in infancy. If no personal faith was required before entering the covenant in those days why now? So runs the argument. It will do us well to examine the differences in the two major covenants of the Bible: that with Israel and that with the church.

Covenant is a basic Bible word. In all covenants there are parties, terms and promises. In contracts between

THERE IS A DIFFERENCE

men, the parties involved may be equals. In the Biblical covenants that God has made with the Jews long ago and the church today, He makes the stipulations and the promises, the people only respond by accepting or rejecting. Note the world of difference between the first and second covenants.

THERE ARE DIFFERENT PARTIES

In covenant number one the parties were God and the Jews, the physical sons of Abraham, Isaac and Jacob. That covenant of old was made with Israel's "fathers in the day" God "took them by the hand to lead them forth out of the land of Egypt" (Heb. 8:9). In other words, the Jews delivered from the Egyptian bondage at the exodus were the people given the covenant. Their offspring became parties to that covenant.

When a child was born to Jewish parents, that child was under the Old Covenant by right of the natural birth. Circumcision of the male foreskin became the mark of being under the covenant. Physical birth to the right parents produced the future members of that covenant people.

Where do we turn today to find salvation? The mediator of the Old Covenant was Moses. The place of its giving was Mount Sinai. The words of the covenant are the ten commandments found in Exodus 20. But we live in the New Testament times. Jesus is the mediator of the New Covenant. Its terms rang forth from apostolic lips first at Mount Zion in Jerusalem, as Peter preached the way of salvation. Acts 2 is more than Exodus 20. Entrance into covenant for us is not national birth by a

Jewish father but spiritual birth by the Heavenly Father.

When one is born a second time, born from above, "born of water and the Spirit," he enters not the kingdom of Israel but the more inclusive kingdom of heaven (cp. John 3:1-7). Where in olden days Canaanites and Philistines were out and but one nation was in, during the church age the covenant is open for all.

This New Testament inclusiveness in no way degrades Jews, for God wants every Jew to be in the New Covenant as well as he was in the Old. The difference is that where there was a limitation in the old, there are no racial or class limitations in the new. One of the better things about this better covenant is that it reaches out to more people.

The New Covenant brings life. The Old Covenant brought death. As you read the lofty ten commandments written on "tables of stone" remember they were called "the ministration of death" (II Cor. 3:7). Each of the commands, when broken, called for the death penalty. An interesting observation is to note the contrast between the opening word of Jesus' Sermon on the Mount and closing word of the Old Testament. Jesus began his message with the word "Blessed" (Matt. 5:3), Malachi ended his final prophecy with the word "curse" (4:6). Since men break God's good laws, they in reality break themselves on them. Disobedient humans find themselves under judgment and condemnation.

Not one man under the Old Covenant was saved by keeping God's laws perfectly. A better way had to be found. More laws would but bring more damnation. People did not need more rules to keep but a Ruler who would keep them. Mankind was in need of a way of salvation that did not depend upon human goodness but upon the goodness of God. Man's works fail. God's work redeems.

Near the mount where God's Old Covenant was given "about three thousand men" perished in punishment for their sin (Exod. 32:28). At the mount where Christ's New Covenant was announced by the apostles, "about three thousand souls" (Acts 2:41) were saved. The symbolism is clear. Paul's Epistle to the Romans is even clearer when it states, "By the works of the law shall no flesh be justified in his (God's) sight; for through the law cometh the knowledge of sin. But now apart from the law a righteousness of God hath been manifested . . . through faith in Jesus Christ" (3:20-22).

Whether you are a Jew or a Gentile matters not. Both "Greeks and . . . Barbarians, both . . . the wise and . . . the foolish" can be in covenant with God in these New Testament times. The Christian gospel is "unto salvation to every one that believeth; to the Jew first, and also to the Greek" (Rom. 1:14-16). Being born a Jew put you in one covenant. Being born again through Jesus places you in the new.

THERE ARE DIFFERENT TERMS

In every covenant there are parties. There are also stipulations or terms. What were the terms of the Old Covenant made at Sinai? They were the ten commandments. God told Israel to keep His law and He gave certain promises based on whether they would, or would not, keep that law. What then are the terms of the New Covenant established by Christ? To answer that question, we need to listen to the author of Hebrews as he speaks of Jesus being "the mediator of a better covenant . . . enacted upon better promises" (8:6).

By quoting the prophecy of Jeremiah that announced the coming "new covenant," the writer clarifies that it will be "not according to the covenant that I (Jehovah) made with their fathers in the day that I took them by the hand to lead them forth out of the land of Egypt" (Heb. 8:9). Any Jew, recalling his history, would know this to be a reference to the ten commandments. It was shortly after the exodus through the sea that Israel received from God at Mount Sinai the covenant that made them God's theocracy.

Where the first covenant was written on tables of stone, the new covenant was to be written "into their mind, And on their heart" (8:10). Paul had referred to the old covenant as "the ministration of death, written and graven on stones." He knew it "came with glory," but he also taught that "it is done away in Christ" (II Cor. 3:7,14).

Today some would say that what was done away was but the rituals and ceremonies of olden days. The apostles, however, did not make such distinctions between moral and ceremonial portions in the law. They saw the entire package brought through Moses, replaced by the covenant mediated by Christ.

Hebrews 8:9 is pointing to the covenant made at the exodus, the ten commandments. That is true to Bible terminology. Read Deuteronomy 4:13: "And he declared unto you his covenant, which he commanded you to perform, even the ten commandments; and he wrote them upon two tables of stone." Ask yourself what the Jews labeled the ark in which they kept the ten commandments. The ark was called "the ark of the covenant." It was so termed because the ten commandments were "the tables of the covenant." The stipulations given to Israel were these ten commandments. The words inscribed on the tables of stone began, "I am Jehovah thy God, who brought thee out of the land of Egypt, out to the house of bondage" (Exod. 20:2). The ten commands that follow are, by this preamble, directed to Israel. Jeremiah and the writer of Hebrews do not identify the ten commands with the new covenant written on new material. They rather announce that they will be "Not according to the covenant . . . made with their fathers" (8:9). The writer of the epistle concludes, "In that he saith, A new covenant, he hath made the first old. But that which is becoming old and waxeth aged is nigh unto vanishing away" (8:13).

The church, God's New Israel, understood that God had "blotted out the bond written in ordinances that was against" them. He did this by "nailing it to the cross" (Col. 2:14). That being true, how were believers to respond to Judaizers who would force the mixing of the law with the gospel? Paul draws a conclusion that sets Christians free. He writes, "Let no man therefore judge you in meat, or in drink, or in respect of a feast day or a new moon or a sabbath day: which are a shadow of the things to come but the body is Christ's" (2:16).

The converts of Paul's first missionary journey were troubled by men from Jerusalem. These insisted that these Gentile converts would need to do more than be believers in Christ and be baptized into him. Paul's Galatian letter asserted that the law was "added because of transgression," was to remain in effect "till the seed (Christ) should come" (3:19). That law was to serve as a "tutor to bring us unto Christ. . . . But now that faith is come, we are no longer under a tutor" (3:24-25). "For the law was given through Moses; grace and truth came through Jesus Christ" (John 1:17). On the mount of transfiguration, Moses and Elijah (representing the law and prophets) are with Jesus. God causes Moses and Elijah to vanish as he acknowledges Jesus as His Son and He distinguishes him from the others by saying, "Hear ye him" (Matt. 17:1-8). The commands through Moses were high commands. Those revealed through Jesus are even higher. What was said by Moses of olden time was good. What is taught by Christ is "better." The contrast with Moses in the Sermon on the Mount is purposeful. "Ye have heard that it was said to them of old time . . . but I say unto you" (Matt. 5:21-22).

If the terms to Israel were to "keep the law," the stipulations for the church are, briefly put, "Live for Jesus." It is as if Jesus said, "I died for you, now you live for me." In simple terminology, Christ-likeness is the believer's requirement. The church is the body of Christ. What he sought to do in the incarnation, we strive to continue in this day. He searched for the lost. He nurtured his followers. Upon our baptism we died to personal ambitions and rose to walk working for his goals. His commission spoke of discipling the nations and teaching the observation of his commands.

THERE ARE DIFFERENT PROMISES

Jesus not only mediated "a better covenant" than

Moses, his agreement was "enacted upon better promises" (Heb. 8:6). One of the ten commands carried with it a promise. "Honor thy father and thy mother, that thy days may be long in the land which Jehovah thy God giveth thee" (Exod. 20:12). God was covenanting with Israel that, if they would go by His laws, there would be for God's people material blessings. He would make them prosper. He would make them great among the nations.

The new covenant moved from an agreement between one nation to a covenant including the world. It progressed from ten just and holy commandments to the even higher commands of Christ. It went from the promise of an earthly homeland to the assurance of a heavenly home. The "many mansions" of eternity, plus life in the presence of God for ever, cause the land of Palestine to appear insignificant.

The preceding verse of the Jeremiah prophecy told of the new time coming when "they shall not teach every man his fellow-citizen, And every man his brother, saying Know the Lord: For all shall know me, From the least to the greatest" (Heb. 8:11). Here is one of the great differences between the two covenants. Under the old, a child born by physical birth into a Jewish family, would not in its earliest days know the Lord until parental teaching brought a consciousness of right and wrong and an awareness of God's nature. In these New Testament times, no one enters covenant with God by natural birth to Jewish or Christian parents. It is rather when a human comes to "know the Lord," then he is in covenant with Christ. Only those who know the Lord (small or big, least or great) are in the kingdom.

No accident of physical birth makes a citizen of heaven. Upon hearing God's invitation, the free will of man can accept or reject the offer. To the responsive persons God's promise comes, their "sins will I remember no more." How different from the days of Sinai to those of Calvary. Animal sacrifice at the Jewish tabernacle and temple could not remove sin. Rather both Passover and the Day of Atonement but rolled ahead the sins of the people until the New Covenant would come and all sins could be removed forever. Under the first covenant sins were remembered. Under the final covenant iniquities are removed.

God signed the new covenant in the blood shed at Mount Calvary. Where do we sign on the dotted line? On the first day of the New Testament church, the apostles of Jesus announced "remission of sins; and . . . the gift of the Holy Spirit" to the believers who would "Repent . . . and be baptized" (Acts 2:38). Peter called that "the promise" (2:39). The three thousand respondents, by that very act, were accepting a covenant of salvation that was by grace and not by race. They were not trusting in the physical birth that was theirs being born of a Jewish father. They were putting their hope in a spiritual birth from above. They were entering the New Covenant. Once again good is good, but better is better. Best of all is Jesus.

CHAPTER THIRTEEN

Who Moved the Furniture?
Hebrews 9:1-10

(The Covenant and Its Design)

I am getting too old to move furniture. More than once I have been reminded of that. Once I chose to live in a condominium at the center of the housing complex. There we would be at a distance from either the traffic noise of the busy street or the joyful noise of children playing at the swimming pool. What I forgot to consider was how far the U-Haul at the nearest curb would be from my front door. It would not have been so bad if my wife played a ukulele, but she played both a piano and organ that had to be carried the equivalent of a city block. I should have remembered trying to move those heavy instruments into an earlier second-floor apartment just off a very narrow stair-case. Moving furniture is an art, especially if the door openings are small and the area of manipulation is practically non-existent.

The topic before us does not deal with moving furniture into a house, but rather with moving furniture within a house, particularly within the house of God.

Being an early riser, I try each morning without benefit of bright lights to slip out of my apartment without waking anybody else in the family. On one day, I well remember, I was attempting the move from the bedroom, down the hall, across the living room and out the front door without the lights on. What had worked all the times before, did not work on that occasion for somebody had moved the furniture around from where I was accustomed for it to be.

Hebrews chapter nine describes the furniture found in the house of God (cp. vv. 1-5). What was there and where it was placed was no accident. God intended it to be "a copy and shadow of the heavenly things." For that reason Moses was warned to "make all things according to the pattern" revealed "in the mount" (8:5). God was particular about the items in the tabernacle for each piece of furniture was to illustrate something for the coming Christian era. New Testament Christians would find in the ancient tabernacle an object lesson for them.

Consider three important questions. Who moved the furniture in? God did. Who moved it out or changed it around? Man did. Who is moving it back where it ought to be? We all ought to try.

GOD MOVED IT IN

Pay attention to what furnishings God placed in and around the tabernacle by design. Learn what those old items foreshadowed for today.

Walk mentally into the tabernacle of old. As you

draw near, the first item you will see is called the "altar of sacrifice." That stands for the cross of Christ, where the Saviour offered himself for the sins of the world. The first thing a person needed to remember, as he came to worship God, was the holiness of his Deity and the sinfulness of his personal life. How can such a sinner go into the presence of the Holy One? Let such a man observe the altar where the blood of an innocent victim has been poured out. That lamb or ox typified that the sinless Son of God could take the place of guilty men vicariously. All worshippers must go to God by "the way of the cross." As the song goes, "There's no other way but this."[1]

The book of Leviticus reminded every priest that "the life of the flesh is in the blood; and I (Jehovah) have given it to you upon the altar to make atonement for your souls: for it is the blood that maketh atonement by reason of the life" (17:11). As Paul defined the gospel, he placed "first of all that . . . Christ died for our sins according to the scriptures" (I Cor. 15:3). Jesus is our "altar" that by his death did "sanctify the people through his own blood" (Heb. 13:10-12).

The person going into the house of God passed first of all the altar of sacrifice that portrayed the cross of Christ. What next came into view was the "sea of brass," commonly known as "the laver" (Exod. 30:18). The priest that offered the sacrifice would next bathe at the laver before he entered the tabernacle proper. The holy place typified the church, as the laver stood for baptism. Paul used the word laver (λουτρόν) in speaking to his Christian workers. He told Titus it "was not by works done in righteousness, which we did ourselves, but according to his (God's) mercy he saved us by the washing (laver) of regeneration and renewing of the Holy Spirit" (3:5). He had earlier told the Ephesians that God had cleansed his church "by the washing (laver) of water with the word" (5:26). Today each believer in Jesus first heard of Christ's sacrifice for his sins. He then passed through the waters of baptism into the church, the temple of God for today. In the typical tabernacle proper you see on the left the candelabrum. That lamp stood for God's revelation. The candelabrum had a major stem and three arms on either side, totaling seven, the number of perfection. Each stem held a vial of oil representing the Holy Spirit as the source of the light.

The baptized believers in the earliest church "continued steadfastly in the apostle's teaching" (Acts 2:42). The Scripture is the only light for God's church, as the candelabrum was the only lamp in the ancient tent of meeting. So the Psalmist sang to God, "Thy word is a lamp unto my feet, and a light unto my path" (119:105). So the Apostle instructed Timothy, "Every scripture inspired of God is profitable . . . for instruction" (II Tim. 3:16).

Where the lamp is to the left, the "table of the presence" is to the right. It was reset with fresh unleavened loaves every seven days (Lev. 24:5-8). There were twelve pieces of unleavened bread to remind of the twelve tribes. Also on the table were cups of wine. Since in New Testament times the church is God's temple, might this not have foretold of the weekly Lord's Supper that marked the Christian gatherings? The bread unleavened calls to mind the life of Christ unleavened with the sin of the world. The cups, filled with the blood of the grape, bring to memory the necessity of Christ's death for us to share in life.

On the way in, we come by the altar of sacrifice and the laver, for "he that believeth and is baptized shall be saved" (Mark 16:16). Once having "received his word" and being "baptized," the redeemed continue in the "teaching . . . the breaking of bread and the prayers" (Acts 2:41-42). "Prayers" are represented in the type by the altar of incense (Psa. 141:2; Rev. 5:8).

The incense was burned right up against the veil that separated the "holy place" from the "holy of holies." Every priest got that far in his worship, but only the high priest could go on Yom Kippur beyond the veil. Yet while the regular priests could not enter the most holy place, the incense could penetrate the curtain. As the aroma of incense went where their eyes could not see, the priest knew his supplications were getting into the presence of God.

The position of the altar of incense next to the curtain has led preachers to observe that the closest any man can come to God today is in prayer. As our nostrils catch the scent of incense, God's ears hear the supplications and praise of his people.

Josephus tells us that the temple's veil was so thick that teams of horses could not have torn it asunder. The material was too strong to be ripped by men. The cubical building was a type of heaven, the city foursquare. Sin, like a veil, separates from God. When Jesus died the veil was rent from the top to bottom, and access to God was now a reality.

Behind the veil stood "the ark of the covenant." In addition to manna and Aaron's rod, this ark held the tables of the covenant. Men must be reminded that the God of heaven had made covenant with men on earth. The manna called to mind that God provided for His covenant people. The rod was to be a reminder that He also leads His covenanted nation.

To review the type and its anti-type, is to recall that we became Christian by faith and baptism and we remain in covenant by the teaching, the communion and prayer. We receive assurance that one day we will go beyond the veil into the presence of God.

MAN MOVED IT OUT

Read again the warning of Hebrews 8:5, "See, saith he, that thou make all things according to the pattern that was showed thee." Human workmen may not know why the architect wanted furnishings to be built like they are or placed where they are. One might think, carelessly, that his opinion is as valid as the blueprint's specification. He might deem it an improvement to move some furniture.

God, by instruction to Moses, moved the furniture into the tabernacle as it pleased Him. Man, by his reasoning, changed some of it about.

To the human mind there seemed to be too much emphasis on the altar of sacrifice and atoning blood. A modernist strain in Christian tradition called for the elimination of what they called butchershop religion. It cut back in the hymnal the songs about blood and the cross.

Others were embarassed by the laver. A variety of ef-

WHO MOVED THE FURNITURE?

forts to move baptism to a less prominent place have occurred. Our paedo-baptist friends put the laver first. They baptize infants who have never heard of the sacrifice of Jesus. The order in the temple was not first the laver, then the sacrificial altar. It was the altar, then the laver.

Other believers preferred to place the laver inside the tabernacle rather than at the entrance. They made baptism something a person inside the church should do, but rejected the legitimacy of considering it something that stands between the cross and church membership.

Mormons put the laver behind the veil and baptize for those beyond the pale of death. Others leave the laver where it is, but drain all the water out of it, leaving what they would call a baptism of the Spirit. Still others put the laver off to the side making it an option, but not a necessity.

The candelabrum was the only light in the original tabernacle, and stood for the Bible as God's only light in the church. Several groups today bring in another book claiming to be light, to supplement the original one. Latter day revelation by a modern prophet or prophetess is taken as truth equal to the apostolic and prophetic word called Scripture. Some even would drill a hole in the ceiling to let in natural light. Then, in addition to the Bible, God could reveal directly to our spirits His truths. As if that were not sufficient, we hear that an opening in the wall would welcome light from the other religions of the world. In this eclectic day this view is gaining popularity.

The Lord's table in the early church, like the foreshadowing table of shewbread, was reset each week.

Voices call for once a quarter or once a month being adequate. They argue a thing done too often becomes just a ritual with little meaning. While none of these advocates would argue this, because such was the early church's practice, they rather give their opinion that too much is too much. A better question, is, "can one find God's opinion?" A serious inquiry ought to be "should regular prayer and Bible study be exchanged for an occasional experience?"

The revivalists, who move the altar of incense outside the tabernacle, use the "sinner's prayer" as the entrance into the tabernacle. "Praying through" has replaced the laver in their instruction. A comparison of their teaching with the apostolic standards set in the book of Acts shows more contrasts than similarities.

WE CAN MOVE IT BACK

Many of us believe that Christian unity can be forwarded by each believer and each congregation returning to the faith and practice of the church at its beginning. If over the centuries of time changes have been made in the basic doctrines or goals, the restudy of the New Testament should help us test if the alterations have been improvements. To be simply Christians rather than party advocates and to consider the apostle's teaching as normative for all time rather than subject to change, seems the way to attract the world to Christ. Human opinions carry little or no authority. "Thus saith the Lord" bears weight to all who consider Jesus to be "Lord and Christ" (Acts 2:36).

WHO MOVED THE FURNITURE?

Since God said, "See . . . that thou make all things according to the pattern" (Heb. 8:5), attention to all His instructions is both wisdom and obedience. Church history tells the embarrassing story of the sectarian divisions. No one who has rearranged the furniture can expect all the others in God's large family to submit to that rearrangement. The best hope is to recognize that God's hand was in the developing church from the beginning. If the Holy Spirit guided Jesus' apostles "into all the truth" (John 16:13), the discovery and acceptance of that revelation should be the primary desire of all who name Christ's name.

It would be most appropriate today to give instruction to seekers as they did in century one: "Repent ye, and be baptized unto the remission of your sins" (Acts 2:38). While the apostles of Jesus guided the spread of the gospel across the world, the proclamation of salvation was to announce the cross (the altar of sacrifice) and then lead the responsive persons to baptism (the laver). Every case of conversion recorded in the book of Acts shows conscious obedience to Christ's instruction: "Go . . . preach the gospel. . . . He that believeth and is baptized shall be saved" (Mark 16:15-16).

The way of salvation was reflected in the furnishing of laver and altar that led into the holy place. The way of worship was typified in the furniture inside that first room in the tabernacle. Regarding the very first additions to the church, the historian Luke declares, "They then that received his word were baptized" (Acts 2:41). Describing their way of worship, he writes, "And they continued steadfastly in the apostles' teaching and fellowship, in the breaking of bread and the prayers"

(2:42). To use Old Testament symbolism, there were candelabra, the table of the presence and the altar of incense.

It appears to be God's will that any furniture man has moved from where He put it by design, ought to be returned to its original place. In some way and to some degree most every piece in the type has been shifted by the preferences and traditions of men. But, there is one item that God himself removed. It is the veil in the temple that heaven tore asunder at Jesus' death. Dividing between the first and second rooms of the temple, it marked the separation between earth and heaven. The sin that had separated man from God was taken away at the cross. Fellowship between man and his Maker was restored. Atonement was accomplished by Jesus' blood.

As Jesus expired upon the cross not only did the temple's veil rend in two, a very discerning earthquake broke open tombs where Jerusalem saints had been buried (cp. Matt. 27:51-53). On the Sunday of Christ's resurrection, these earlier believers also walked again the streets of the holy city. God was demonstrating in Jerusalem the relationship between Christ's death and resurrection and the believer's access to God's presence beyond the veil.

Endnotes

1. Jessie B. Pounds, "The Way of the Cross Leads Home," *Favorite Hymns of Praise* (Wheaton, IL: Tabernacle Publishing Co., 1967), p. 402.

CHAPTER FOURTEEN

Where There's A Will, There's A Way
Hebrews 9:11-22

(The Covenant as Testament)

Have you ever been remembered in a will? Your Bible says you have indeed! Because of Christ's "eternal redemption" (Heb. 9:12) offered through his "eternal Spirit" (9:14), you now have "promise of the eternal inheritance" (9:15). You have become heir of God through the last will and testament of our Lord Jesus Christ. Because of that will, there is a way.

Many a college has been able to do what otherwise would have been impossible, because the school was remembered in someone's will. Many a person possesses a car, or a house, or a bank account by the boost given them at the death of a person that, believing in them, wrote their name as an heir.

A long time ago someone died and left you a fortune. That someone was Jesus. The author of Hebrews writes significant things about this will in chapter nine, especially in verses 16-17. He says, "For where a testament is, there must of necessity be the death of him that made it. For a testament is of force where there hath been death: for it doth never avail while he that made it liveth."

THE WILL BEHIND THE WILL

When a written will is drawn up, you know there has been a will behind that will. A person has determined, or willed, how he wants his possessions distributed. The human will precedes the written will. The written will never goes into effect until the death of the one that made it.

For many years Hebrews 9:16-17 has been a help in my personal ministry. When people have been troubled over the difference in covenants, I would open to this passage of Scripture. It became an easy matter to point out that Jesus lived under the old covenant and that his new covenant did not come into effect until after he died. If the parishioner was asking why Jesus went on Saturday to worship in the synagogue while the Christian Church gathers on Sunday, this Bible passage furnished the answer. Christ observed the Sabbaths in the local synagogues and the annual Passovers in the temple for he was "born under the law" (Gal. 4:4). That old covenant did not expire until Jesus' death. His disciples from Pentecost on followed Christ's will that went into effect after his death.

When some person raised the issue that the thief on the cross was taken into Paradise and yet was not asked to be baptized, they were wanting to know why churches today call for both faith and baptism. Again

WHERE THERE'S A WILL, THERE'S A WAY

Hebrews 9:16-17 was a handy text for dissolving the seeming discrepancy. A person gives his possessions to whom he will. After his death, they are recipients who meet the terms of the will. A will goes into effect only after the death of its maker. It was following Jesus' death and resurrection that he gave the commission to be followed "unto the end of the world" (Matt. 28:20). In that instruction Jesus called for the discipling and baptizing of the nations. That is the will that missionaries and evangelists are to follow. To the church the models of salvation and worship are not the practice under the former covenant of Sinai but the better covenant that followed. We teach the gospel both lived and proclaimed by the Spirit-inspired apostles who carried out Jesus' bidding after his death.

To be faithful to the author of Hebrews we need to view this shorter text of 9:1-17 in the running argument from the opening chapter 1. The writer is affirming that everything in the New Covenant is "better" than what was in the Old. Indeed God spoke in olden days through prophets and angels, yet Christ is a "better messenger" (ch. 1-2). In those earlier times Jehovah raised up deliverers like Moses and Joshua, but Jesus' deliverance exceeds theirs (ch. 3-4). Long ago there was the priesthood of Aaron and Melchizedek; however, the eternal priesthood of the Lord is far "better" in many ways (ch. 5-7). Then chapters 8 and 9 continue the contrast of Christianity to Judaism, proclaiming the covenant brought by Christ to be "better" than that which preceded it. This new testament, of which the author speaks, came into force after "the death of him that made it" (9:16).

BEST OF ALL IS JESUS

Behind every will that is written stands the personal will of its maker. That is true regarding the last will and testament of the Lord Jesus Christ. We often speak of the will of God. Any promises you read in the written New Testament are there because in the will of God is your salvation. If you are ever remembered in somebody's will, it must mean that this person thought about you. That individual cared about you. That man or woman chose to give you something that you never could otherwise have possessed. It was to be considered a gift, or a blessing, from the donor. To be included in Christ's will makes certain that we are not insignificant to him.

That Jesus cares about us is clear from the Sermon on the Mount. He speaks of walking on the lilies of the field that are more glorious than Solomon's finest garb. He concludes, "if God doth so clothe the grass of the field, which today is, and tomorrow is cast into the oven, shall he not much more clothe you?" (Matt. 6:30). If grass or sparrows are important to the heavenly Father, "Are not ye of much more value than they?" (6:26). The songwriter, Civilla D. Martin, cannot be wrong when he sings "His eye is on the sparrow, And I know He watches me." We are not mistaken when we ask "Does Jesus Care?" and we answer "O yes, He cares; I know He cares, His heart is touched with my grief."[1] The choir is right when they hymn, "No one ever cared for me like Jesus."[2]

Your name is recorded in the last will and testament of Jesus Christ. That means he cares for you. You have "the promise of the eternal inheritance" (Heb. 9:15). What does that include? A moment with a Bible Concor-

WHERE THERE'S A WILL, THERE'S A WAY

dance will help you find promises containing the words "inherit, inheritance, heir, etc."

"Come, ye blessed of my Father, inherit the kingdom prepared for you from the foundation of the world" (Matt. 25:34). "Fear not, little flock; for it is your Father's good pleasure to give you the kingdom" (Luke 12:32). We know that the "unrighteous shall not inherit the kingdom of God . . . but ye were washed" (I Cor. 6:9-11). Part of our inheritance in Christ is the eternal kingdom of heaven. But there is more. "Every one that hath left houses, or brethren, or sisters, or father, or mother, or children, or lands, for my name's sake, shall receive a hundred-fold, and shall inherit eternal life" (Matt. 19:29). The inheritance is the kingdom. The inheritance is eternal life. And, according to the beatitude, "the meek . . . shall inherit the earth" (Matt. 5:5).

Earlier in Hebrews we learned that angels are "all ministering spirits, sent forth to do service for the sake of them that shall inherit salvation" (1:14). As we begin to add the lengthening list of what we shall inherit, we find it includes the kingdom, the earth, life and salvation. And the list goes on, for we are "heirs of God, and joint-heirs with Christ" (Rom. 8:17), because we are His children. Let each heart sing:

> My Father is rich in houses and lands, He holdeth the wealth of the world in His hands! Of rubies and diamonds, of silver and gold, His coffers are full, He has riches untold.
>
> I once was an outcast stranger on earth, A sinner by choice, and an alien by birth; But I've been adopted, my name's written down, An heir to a mansion, a robe, and a crown. I'm a child of the king . . . [3]

Rejoice with Paul for "all things are yours; whether . . . the world, or life, or death, or things present, or things to come; all are yours; and ye are Christ's; and Christ is God's" (I Cor. 3:21-23). Behind a will is a will. God the Father has willed that all who accept His Son inherit every blessing.

THE TEST BEHIND THE TESTAMENT

Was the testament of our Lord Jesus Christ made properly? Was it recorded correctly? When challenged by our adversary the Devil, will it stand his assaults?

In the upper room on the night before he died, Jesus spoke: "This is my blood of the (new) covenant, which is poured out for many unto remission of sins" (Matt. 26:28. We might say Christ is signing that testament in his own blood. He guarantees the promise.

The last will and testament was made correctly, but was it recorded properly? The ambassadors of the Lord were promised, "Whatsoever thou shalt bind on earth shall be bound in heaven; and whatsoever thou shalt loose on earth shall be loosed in heaven" (Matt. 16:19). As the witnesses of the gospel, the apostles spoke and wrote "as the Spirit gave them utterance" (Acts 2:4). We can rely on their words.

In the Greek of Matthew 16:19 we find the future perfect periphrastic. This means that what Peter and his fellow apostles say on earth "shall have been bound in heaven." In other words, it is not because the apostles said something, that it was to become the standard. Rather, because Christ already had made it the standard in heaven, that is what the apostles spoke. The promised Holy Spirit did "guide" them to utter "all the truth" (John 16:13).

Our testament stands the test. Jesus signed it in his own blood. The apostles recorded it under inspiration. Will the adversary, the Devil, be able to challenge it before the court of the universe? God's Bible hurls out the challenge, "Who shall lay anything to the charge of God's elect? It is God that justifieth. . . . Who shall separate us from the love of Christ? Shall tribulation, or anguish, or persecution, or famine, or nakedness, or peril, or sword? . . . Nay, in all these things we are more than conquerors through him that loved us" (Rom. 8:33-37).

Since a testament is never in effect until the death of its maker, has Jesus already died for our sins? Since the answer is yes, then the will is now in force. It has passed every test.

THE INHERITOR BEHIND THE INHERITANCE

Behind the will is God's personal will. Behind the testament is the test. This new testament of our Lord Jesus Christ passes all its tests with flying colors. We now note that in the word "inheritance" is implied an "inheritor."

The very first evangelistic meeting in which I shared leadership, I was song leader and instrumentalist in Milwaukie, Oregon. B. Ross Evans was evangelist for the State of Oregon and effectively used charts in his teaching. I recall the large canvas chart he had on the subject of inheritance. Brother Evans told of a will where a grandfather was providing for his children's children. According to the terms of the will any one of these grandchildren would inherit on or after they reached the age of twenty one, provided that they were married and resided in the State of Iowa. Going through the chart the evangelist told of one grandchild who lived in Iowa but was not married, of another who was of proper age but had left the state, and so on. The point being pressed home was that to inherit a person had to meet all the requirements of the will.

Folding the chart in a special way, the evangelist then revealed a check-list of the terms Jesus gave in the great commission accounts. Both there and in the conversion stories of Acts he showed such words as "believe," "repent" and "be baptized." The listeners were assured that they were in on the inheritance of Christ if they met its clear stipulations.

The "whosoevers" of Scripture indicate whose names are included in the list of heirs. John 3:16 heads the list. It tells of the love of God shown to all in the giving of His only begotten Son. It promises "that whosoever believeth on him should not perish, but have eternal life." This is not a "whosoever" that takes in all who dwell on the earth. It draws into its circle everyone of the earth-dwellers that believe in Jesus. If you are a believer you have met one requirement for a name to be "enrolled in heaven" (Heb. 12:23).

Matthew 10:32 records another "whosoever," that includes "every one" that shall "confess" Christ before men. These will be the ones Jesus will confess before his Father. You too are in on the inheritance, if you are a believer who openly confesses that Jesus is the Christ. You are included in the "whosoevers," when you are doing what the verb says that follows each of these pronouns. We have met "whosoever believeth" and "whosoever confesseth" Christ.

Acts 2:21 promises salvation to "whosoever shall call on the name of the Lord." This is the beginning of Peter's sermon. At the end of that message crowds are calling, "what shall we do?" (2:37). The inspired preacher's answer included baptism, for that was the God-ordained way to call on the name of the Lord (cp. 2:38). So it was with Saul of Tarsus. He was told after his coming to faith not to tarry, but to "arise, and be baptized, and wash away . . . sins, calling on his name" (Acts 22:16). This passage suggests that baptism is a prayer. The believing sinner, as he is buried beneath the wave, is calling on the name of the Lord for the salvation promised to those who so call. I Peter 3:21 speaks of a salvation through water, calling "baptism . . . the interrogation of a good conscience toward God." This "interrogation," or asking, or appeal or inquiry, is the prayer of the convert, as he calls on the name of the Lord.

Does a man have to believe? Must he confess? Is it a necessity he be baptized? Write it down that man has been given a free will. All are invited to "Come," but the invitation is to "whosoever will" (Rev. 22:17, KJV). The benefits are not offered to "whosoever won't," but to "whosoever will."

Back to our basic text in Hebrews. There chapter 9:18-22 speaks of the old covenant. Since a testament is not in force until after death, what death preceded the old covenant? Jesus' death was before the new testament came into power, but how was it in the earlier testament with Israel? Our author points to "the blood of the calves and the goats." These typologically died, symbolizing Jesus' coming death. Their blood initiated the preparatory covenant that anticipated the Messiah's sacrifice which in turn would inaugurate the eternal covenant.

The Lamb of God has died for the sins of the world. The New Testament of God's grace is in effect. Since the will of God is behind that will and testament, are you willing to be willed into the riches of eternity? Since the testament has been tested and found secure, are you ready to pass the test? Are you answering "yes" to each item the apostolic circle made "binding on earth?" Can you aver that you are an "heir?" Do you agree with Paul? He wrote, "For ye are all sons of God, through faith in Christ Jesus. For as many of you as were baptized into Christ did put on Christ. . . . And if ye are Christ's, then are ye Abraham's seed, heirs according to promise" (Gal. 3:26-29).

Endnotes

    1. Frank E. Graeff, "Does Jesus Care?" *Favorite Hymns of Praise*, (Wheaton, IL: Tabernacle Publishing Co., 1967), p. 384.
    2. C.F. Weigle, *Christian Service Songs* (Winona Lake, IN: The Rodeheaver-Hall Mack, Co., 1939), p. 57.
    3. Harriet E. Buell, "A Child of the King," *Favorite Hymns of Praise* (Wheaton, IL: Tabernacle Publishing Co., 1967), p. 210.

CHAPTER FIFTEEN

Waiting for the Second Coming
Hebrews 9:23-28

(The Covenant and Its Once-for-all-ness)

"**O**nce upon a time" is the way a fairy tale begins. It is not the wording often used to launch a Scriptural study. The Bible is based on established fact and not upon fable. Yet an examination of Hebrews 9 can well begin with the phrase "once in time." That chapter reminds the reader that some events of history occurred once-for-all. Jesus' incarnation happened one time. He died on Calvary and rose from the dead but once. As surely as there is but "one body . . . one Spirit . . . one hope . . . one Lord, one faith, one baptism" and "one God" (Eph. 4:4-6), there is to be one second coming.

Several times in Hebrews 9 you have read the word "once" or "once for all." Five times in the single chapter you have noted its appearance at verse 7, 12, 26, 27 and 28. But at the end of these occurrences of "once," "once for all," "once at the end of the ages," "once to die" and "once offered," comes the promise that our

High Priest "shall appear a second time, apart from sin, to them that wait for him, unto salvation" (9:28). This is a clear announcement of Christ's second coming. Having done his previous ministry of incarnation, sacrifice and conquest of death perfectly, there will be no need to repeat those events again in human history. That one time was all sufficient.

SECOND COMING

The text before us affirms a second coming of Jesus. That awaited event has been the blessed-hope of Christ's disciples ever since he ascended to the Father. It has been reaffirmed in all major creeds of Christendom. Those statements of faith aver that Jesus was born of the Virgin Mary, crucified under Pontius Pilate, raised again on the third day and will come again to judge the world.

The glorious hope of the Lord's return is not only basic to the creeds of the church but also basic to its hymns. Believers sing the words of Fanny J. Crosby, "Let us hope and trust, let us watch and pray, And labor till the Master comes."[1] A favorite song today is "The King Is Coming."[2]

The New Testament teaches that Jesus will return visibly. As he went away visibly, he will return "in like manner as . . . beheld . . . going into heaven" (Act 1:11). As he ascended to be enveloped in a cloud, he will so return "with the clouds; and every eye shall see him" (Rev. 1:7). He will return in glory. He will come back in a twinkling of an eye at the last trump. But, come back he will.

That return taught in the Scriptures will not be to die again for our sins. He has already died for your salvation and his return will be to raise you from the dead, to judge all men and to return the kingdom to his Father on whose behalf he has been reigning in conquest. As Paul envisioned our resurrection, he spoke of Christ's resurrection as "the firstfruits" and that of those belonging to him as the harvest to occur "at his coming." He added, "Then cometh the end, when he shall deliver up the kingdom to God, even the Father" (I Cor. 15:23-24).

SECOND CHRISTMAS

If we were all voting on the topic, we would cast a "yes" vote for the second coming. No other vote could be given in the light of Hebrews 9:28, "Christ also . . . shall appear a second time."

The writer and readers knew the practice of Old Testament High Priests. Annually on Yom Kippur, the Day of Atonement, the High Priest would do what no ordinary priest could do. He would take the blood shed at the altar of sacrifice into the Holy of Holies beyond the veil. There he would apply the blood. The Israelites encamped round about would be waiting their High Priest's return into view. All the time he was unseen behind the veil, the people were concerned. How could any human stand in the presence of the Holy One? The High Priest's attire included bells worn close to his feet, so even when he was beyond any man's vision, his movement could be heard. The people could know he was alright, even though unseen. They kept waiting for their High Priest to return through the veil that separated. They awaited the blessing he would give them upon his return.

Christ, our High Priest, has not gone behind the veil of the earthly temple. He, rather, has gone beyond our view into heaven itself. There he appears before the heavenly Father on our behalf. As the new Israel, the church lives in anticipation of his return. Like the tribes of old, we know he will return a second time.

At the second coming we will not have a second Christmas. That incarnation of long ago was for God to take on a body of flesh in order that He later could die in our stead at Calvary. Think of that first coming and how quietly God invaded history. We sing, "O little town of Bethlehem, How still we see thee lie!" We carol its verse, "How silently, how silently, the wondrous Gift is giv'n! So God imparts to human hearts the blessings of His Heav'n."[3] Our favorite Christmas song is "Silent Night, holy night, All is calm, all is bright."[4]

At the first advent how few in the world knew about it. Bethlehem, as the prophet said, was "little to be among the thousands of Judah" (Micah 5:2). A few of its shepherds were informed of the birth of the world's Saviour. The virgin Mary in the stable that night practically was an unknown. But, God knew his Son was entering the world this first time to deal with the sin problem. How different it will be when he comes again. As the author writes, he "shall appear a second time, apart from sin." That is, the first coming was for the purpose of dealing with sin. Not so, will be the second coming.

When Christ returns to earth, the angelic choir will

not be announcing, "There is born to you this day in the city of David a Saviour, who is Christ the Lord" (Luke 2:11). Instead, Jesus will be coming as King of kings and Lord of Lords. The first coming was a quiet coming. The second coming will be accompanied "with a shout, with the voice of the archangel, and with the trump of God" (I Thess. 4:16). The initial coming was known to very few, the final coming will be known to all, for "as the lightning cometh forth from the east, and is seen even unto the west; so shall be the coming of the Son of man" (Matt. 24:27). On that crowning day "every eye shall see him" (Rev. 1:7).

SECOND CALVARY

In the light of Hebrews 9:23-28 it is time to vote again. We must vote "yes" regarding the second coming, but "no" as to there being a second Christmas. We are ready to mark the ballot on the question, "Will there be a second Calvary?"

Hebrews underscores the apostolic teaching that Jesus died once for all. Earthly high-priests brought annually the blood of goats and calves into the holy place. Our High Priest "entered in once for all into the holy place having obtained eternal redemption" (9:12). Jesus did not have to suffer year by year "but now once at the end of the ages . . . put away sin by the sacrifice of himself" (9:26). At Calvary he was "once offered to bear the sins of many" (9:8). He offered but "one sacrifice for sins forever" (10:12).

Century after century, year after year, sacrifice after

sacrifice, animal blood but pointed to the sacrificial lamb God would one day provide. No sin of any size could be handled by lamb, oxen or bullocks. "For it is impossible that the blood of bulls and goats should take away sin" (10:4). Each year but reminded the Israelite that sins were rolled ahead to be faced in the future. Like an insurmountable mountain of debt, sin loomed before each Jew waiting for the One who would come to pay the debt in full. Each tabernacle or temple service of the past was a reminder that God's Messiah had not yet made the adequate sacrifice. Once that offering was given, there would remain no need for another. This is the point the author of Hebrews is making. For a Christian Jew to revert to Judaism, was to turn from the only one who can save and turn back to a system that totally failed to handle the problem of sin.

The church of Jesus Christ knows that "the blood of Jesus his Son cleanseth us from all sin" (I John 1:7). His adequacy replaces the inadequacy under the old regime. We have cast our ballots correctly. There will be no second Calvary, no second death of the messiah on a cross. "Jesus paid it all" is more than a song. It is a Bible fact.

We are well advised to speak as the Scriptures speak. The observance of the Lord's Supper in remembrance of Jesus' death ought not be called "the sacrifice of the mass." No one should suggest by his terminology that Jesus needs to suffer each day for the sins of that day. When God's lamb, Jesus, died for our sins, that one gracious act was abundantly powerful to handle all sin from the time of Adam to the last man to be born on earth. Our communion observance is to proclaim that once-for-all death and participate in its benefits, but not to sacrifice him again.

For this very reason a cross speaks a truer message than a crucifix. The crucifix portrays Jesus still on the cross. The empty cross tells the fuller gospel. Indeed God's Son died on the cruel cross twenty centuries ago. Let that glorious truth ever be preached. But, let it be remembered that he is neither still on the cross nor yet in the tomb. As risen and ascended Lord, he now reigns at God's right hand.

SECOND COMMUNITY

I hope you will vote carefully another time. There will be a second coming, but is there a second community? Today, many teachers who specialize in prophecy lay heavy emphasis on happenings in the Mid-east. To them the return of Jews to Palestine has preaching priority. They consider modern Israel as God's special people in our time. We are told that Jerusalem is the city to rivet our attention at this hour. We are assured that the Jews to this very hour remain God's chosen people. To these dear brethren, often dubbed Dispensationalists, there will be two second comings, two resurrections, two judgements, etc. But more, there are two peoples with whom God is in covenant: the church and the Jewish nation. Both are God's communities, they say.

We all cast our ballot in the private voting booth of our heart. How anyone votes is his personal business. But, as in any election, we ought to study the issues before we mark our ballots. The writings of the Apostles of Christ on this subject are worthwhile reading.

Many of the physical descendants of Abraham, Isaac and Jacob rejected their Messiah. As John put it, "He came unto his own, and they that were his own received him not" (John 1:11). Matthew tells of Jesus' tearful prayer at the end of his earthly ministry:

> O Jerusalem, Jerusalem, that killeth the prophets, and stoneth them that are sent unto her! How often would I have gathered thy children together, even as a hen gathereth her chickens under her wing, and ye would not! Behold, your house is left unto you desolate (Matt. 23:37-38).

The apostle then recalls Jesus' prediction that the Jewish temple would be demolished with not "one stone upon another" (24:2).

There is no question that God chose the Jews as the people through whom His Messiah would come to the world. The only question is whether they remain God's covenant people in unbelief, or whether the church composed of believers from every race is now the Israel of God.

Since there is one Shepherd is there to be one flock? "One flock, one shepherd" is Jesus' answer (John 10:16). Paul gives the "Amen," when he writes, "There is one body" (Eph. 4:4), one church. This community is spiritual Israel. Its connection with Abraham is not physical genealogy but similar faith.

Converts to Christ from the Gentile world are termed by the apostle to the uncircumcision, "the Israel of God" (Gal. 6:16). So that there remain no question, hear Paul's words to some who were former pagans from Antioch, Iconium, Lystra and Derbe:

> For ye are all sons of God, through faith in Christ Jesus. For as many of you as were baptized into Christ did put on Christ. There can be neither Jew or Greek . . . for ye all are one man in Christ Jesus. And if ye are Christ's, then are ye Abraham's seed, heirs according to promise (Gal. 3:26-27).

Physical sons of Abraham are only true sons of Abraham, if they believe in Jesus Christ.

Perhaps you remember the statement of Romans 11:26, "and so all Israel shall be saved." The "so" in this verse must not be taken to mean "therefore," but rather "thus," or "in this manner." Paul has just written that Gentiles were not a part of the natural branch, but by conversion to Christ were grafted into God's olive tree. Jews by disbelief were broken off. That rejection need not be final. They can, "in the same manner" that Gentiles have been put into Christ, be brought into God's community once more by faith in His Son (cp. Rom. 8:15-27). Believing Jews and believing Gentiles constitute one community, not two.

SECOND CHANCE

Tucked away in Hebrews 9:27 is one final question. While there will be a second coming, will there be a second chance? This verse says, "It is appointed unto men to die, and after this comes judgment."

The teaching is that each of us gets to pass through this world but one time. Every person will die one day. After that one death will be judgment. There will be no starting over again in another world. There will be no reincarnation into this world. At death judgment will follow. It will be based upon what we have done in our one life with Jesus and his offer to save.

Hope for an illusory second chance is shattered by Jesus' words to the unprepared and foolish virgins, "and the door was shut" (Matt. 25:10). Later pleas, tears and efforts did not change the verdict. After death shuts the door of opportunity it opens not again. But, while there is life there is hope. How good to know that "now is the acceptable time . . . now is the day of salvation" (II Cor. 6:2).

There will be a second coming. On that day it will be too late to receive Jesus as Saviour, for the day of salvation is "now" and not "then." You likely have had opportunities before to accept the gospel. There may be future occasions when you could make a decision for Christ. But none are guaranteed. What we both know for certain is that nothing stands in the way at this moment, if you are willing.

Endnotes

1. "To the Work!" *Favorite Hymns of Praise* (Wheaton, IL: Tabernacle Publishing Co., 1967), p. 363.
2. *Hymns for the Family of God* (Nashville: Paragon Associates, Inc., 1976), p. 313.
3. Phillip Brooks, "O Little Town of Bethlehem" *Favorite Hymns of Praise* (Wheaton, IL: Tabernacle Publishing Co., 1967), p. 82.
4. Joseph Mohr, "Silent Night! Holy Night!" *Favorite Hymns of Praise* (Wheaton, IL: Tabernacle Publishing Co., 1967). p. 87.

CHAPTER SIXTEEN

When God Forgets
Hebrews 10:1-25

(The Covenant and Forgiveness)

To suggest that God forgets sounds like blasphemy. We rather speak of His omniscience and call our Creator the All-knowing One. Men become senile and forgetful. It is a mark of aging among mortals. But, surely such a trait can never be ascribed to Deity.

God knows our thoughts before we express them. There is nothing we can hide from Him whose eyes are as penetrating as flames of fire. The many prophecies of Old and New Testament reveal a God that declares "the end from the beginning, and from ancient times things that are not yet done" (Isa. 46:10).

As factual as all this is, there is a further glorious truth to which the Holy Spirit pointed in the book of Jeremiah and the fulfillment of which is acknowledged in the book of Hebrews.

> And the Holy Spirit also beareth witness to us; for after he hath said, This is the covenant I will make with them.

After those days, saith the Lord: I will put my laws on their heart, And upon their mind also will I write them; then saith he, And their iniquities will I remember no more (Heb. 10:16-17).

The context argues the need of "a remembrance made of sins year by year" (10:3), in that "it is impossible that the blood of bulls and goats should take away sin" (10:4). Yet the imperfect sacrifices of the old covenant have been taken away. Under the new covenant "we have been sanctified through the offering of the body of Jesus Christ" (10:10). By that one offering Jesus has "perfected for ever them that are sanctified" (10:14).

We can learn an important truth here. God-likeness includes the ability to forget some things. Men, because of their imperfect love, find it next to impossible to forgive people who have done them wrong. They can not get out of their system the fact that they were wronged. They may even claim that they have forgiven the offender, but they will not forget.

How omnipotent is the love of God! We are acquitted, vindicated, justified. Christ's perfect sacrifice meets the law's every demand. Under Jesus' blood our evils are erased. Our "sins and iniquities" are forgiven and forgotten. They will be remembered "no more" (Heb. 10:17).

Upon announcing again this wonderful, redeeming fact, the author of Hebrews calls for a grateful threefold response. Three times he uses the phrase "let us" (10:22,23,24) to introduce what we must never forget, since God has forgotten our sins.

FORGET NOT YOUR BOLDNESS

Immediately after proclaiming that our past sins have

been forgotten, the writer spells out a "therefore." He appeals for our prayers to flow boldly before the throne of God. "Having therefore, brethren, boldness to enter into the holy place by the blood of Jesus . . . let us draw near with a true heart in fulness of faith, having our hearts sprinkled from an evil conscience" (10:19-22). The source of our boldness to come before the Holy One in prayer is the past experience of every Christian. Jesus' blood has had sufficient power to wash away each sin and its stain.

The "sprinkling" referred to here is not of water upon the head, but of the cleansing blood of the Lamb upon our "hearts." Peter also wrote of the "sprinkling of the blood of Jesus Christ" (I Pet. 1:2), saying "ye were redeemed, not with corruptible things, with silver or gold, from your vain manner of life handed down from your fathers; but with precious blood, as of a lamb without blemish and without spot, even the blood of Christ" (1:18-19).

Those that one day rise from the world of tribulation to the peace of eternity, have "washed their robes, and made them white in the blood of the Lamb" (Rev. 7:14). No spots remain for "the blood of Jesus . . . cleanseth us from all sin" (I John 1:7). The grand gospel is that "though your sins be as scarlet, they shall be as white as snow; though they be red like crimson, they shall be as wool" (Isa. 1:18). Hebrews 10 calls for bold prayer not only because of what has happened within our "hearts," but what has been the experience of our "bodies." In the temple the altar of sacrifice stood just before the laver, where the priest would bathe in its water.

Each follower of Christ experienced "the blood of

sprinkling that speaketh better than Abel" (Heb. 12:24). He also knew of the laver of baptism (cp. Eph. 5:26; Titus 3:5), where his "body" was "washed with pure water" (Heb. 10:22). In New Testament times it is safe to say that in a sense baptism was sprinkling, pouring and immersion all at the same time. While in water the body was "buried therefore with him (Christ) through baptism" (Rom. 6:4), the heart was "sprinkled from an evil conscience" by the "blood of Jesus" (Heb. 10:2,19) and the oil of the Holy Spirit was poured out from heaven to anoint God's new servant.

Being "washed . . . sanctified . . . justified in the name of the Lord Jesus Christ, and in the Spirit of our God" (I Cor. 6:7), we ought to boldly enter the "Holy Place" of prayer. With John we should realize, "This is the boldness which we have toward him, that, if we ask anything according to his will, he heareth us" (I John 5:14). After all, God's throne is a "throne of grace" that we are to approach "with boldness" (Heb. 4:16). After all, beyond the veil is the "mercy seat." Are you hesitant to walk into the presence of the King? Remember that you are not a stranger. You are the child of the King. Are you fearful of standing before the Holy One? If you have dealt with your sins according to the teaching of Christ, God has forgotten your iniquities. You remember to be bold in prayer.

FORGET NOT YOUR BELIEFS

Shopping for groceries to feed the body, you may purchase a few heads of lettuce. To feed the soul, we are feasting rather on admonitions that begin "let us." The first was "let us draw near" — a call to prayer. The next is "let us hold fast the confession of our hope that it waver not" (10:23) — a call to persistence. It is good to be reminded that we are in covenant with God. He will never break His vow to us. Since "it is impossible for God to lie, we may have a strong encouragement" (Heb. 6:18). He will keep faith with us. No promise from Him will fail. "He is faithful that promised" (6:12). Should our confession "waver"?

In the first century of the church, along with baptism was the accompanying pledge of allegiance to Christ called the "good confession." Young Timothy was reminded by the apostle how he "didst confess the good confession in the sight of many witnesses," the same "good confession" uttered by Jesus "before Pontius Pilate" (I Tim. 6:12-13). The baptism of the Ethiopian Eunuch was preceded by his declaration "I believe that Jesus Christ is the Son of God" (Acts 8:37, KJV). The early Christians had no creed but Christ. But, every believer pledged allegiance to Jesus as Lord. On that confessed truth the church is, was and will be built (cp. Matt. 16:16-18).

In an earlier chapter our author calls on his readers to "consider the apostle and High Priest of our confession, even Jesus" (3:1). He now begs them to "hold fast the confession" (10:23). They had to decide at the beginning to follow Jesus. Will they now go back on their pledge? Will their audible words as they accept Christ at this later hour be proven empty words? Let none in the church "waver." Hope is lost when faith is lost. "Hold fast" is the strengthening call.

FORGET NOT YOUR BROTHERS

To help any person showing signs of weakening under pressure, the word goes out to draw near to their God in prayer, to hold fast to their convictions with steadfastness and to be considerate of their brothers facing the same trials. "Let us consider one another" begins the third appeal. No one lives or dies unto himself. Every life intertwines with that of others. For one person to accept Jesus as Lord will have a snow-ball effect. Andrew will influence Peter for Christ. Peter will bring his family to the Lord, to say nothing of the thousands that will be affected by his lifelong witness. Yet, the reverse is true as well. Should one "waver" and then "fall away," it would not stop there. Others would take the same road of least resistance. Hence, the plea, "let us consider one another." We are our brother's keepers.

In place of a harmful bad example, become a stimulating help. Encourage the others. "Provoke (one another) unto love and good works" (10:24). Each person can block the way and keep others out of heaven, or they can call for right decisions that lead to life. They can incite others to the actions God desires. They can arouse in fellow-workers the proper feelings and attitudes toward the kingdom.

Of highest impact for good is the consistent example of faithful attendance on the Lord's Day. So the author adds, "not forsaking our own assembling together, as the custom of some is, but exhorting one another" (10:25). On top of inciting others to noble actions of love and good works there ought to be the worshipping together of the people of God.

WHEN GOD FORGETS

From the beginning of the church "upon the first day of the week" disciples of Christ "gathered together to break bread" (Acts 20:7). Individual threads snap easily, but when bound together they have the strength of a rope. Those who followed the Lord did not each go their separate ways; they congregated together for work and worship. They only missed blessing and found judgment when they "discerned not the body" (I Cor. 11:29). They were "many members, but one body" (12:20). Hands, eyes, feet belong together. They were meant for each other. Therefore, let them and "let us" assemble and exhort each other.

Let us also remember "the day drawing nigh" (10:25). To the recipients of the original copy of Hebrews, that day was exceptionally close, but they may not have realized it. Here were some Jewish believers thinking of returning to Judaism, its temple and priesthood. Christ had wept over Jerusalem's coming fall and Israel's dispersion. He had suggested its imminence with the words, "Verily I say unto you, This generation shall not pass away, till all these things be accomplished" (Matt. 24:34). Forty years later, just one or two years after the Hebrew letter, not "one stone upon another" (Matt. 24:2) was left standing. The temple was no more. The literal observance of the Old Covenant had become an impossibility.

Under the New Covenant, as Jeremiah had prophesied, sins, adequately atoned for, were remembered no more by God. No string was tied around His finger to bring before His mind what had been completely forgotten because of Calvary. In gratitude for such grace, we, the freely-forgiven church, ought to remember to hold on to our boldness, our beliefs, and our brothers. Are you praying with boldness? Are you persevering in your faith? Are you provoking love and good works from your fellows? You are invited to come into the body and know partnership and support. The ways of men lead to destruction. Christ's way leads to security. Take the best way — the way of Jesus.

CHAPTER SEVENTEEN

We Shrink Not Back
Hebrews 10:26-39

(The Covenant and Human Choices)

"**B**eautiful" is the appropriate word for Bible passages like the Lord's Prayer and the Shepherd's Psalm. It is not the fitting word for Hebrews 10:26-39. Of all the Scripture verses from the first of Genesis to the last of Revelation, few create more fear than these lines from Hebrews.

A topical preacher or teacher might pass this body of Scripture by, and turn to a part of the Bible that sounds more pleasing to human ears. Expository preachers take texts as they come, under the conviction that what they might deem insignificant could be of great importance to God. Declaring "the whole counsel of God" draws us now to consider this ominous text of Hebrews 10. Jesus in the wilderness recalled the words of Moses, "Man shall not live by bread alone, but by every word that proceedeth out of the mouth of God" (Matt. 4:4; Deut. 8:3).

"If we sin wilfully after that we have received the knowledge of the truth, there remaineth no more a sacrifice for sins but a certain fearful expectation of judgment, and a fierceness of fire which shall devour the adversaries" (Heb. 10:26-27). These words are written to Jews who had come to a knowledge of Jesus as the Messiah and who had accepted him as their Saviour. Now, because of persecution against Christians, they are tempted to leave the Christian church and return to Judaism. The words written so long ago to this specific group remain appropriate for any modern believer considering turning back from the faith.

Follow the logic of the author. In his book he has presented to his readers the unfathomable love of God. Now he declares the possibility of their committing an unpardonable sin which carries the consequence of the unquenchable fire. What is the unreasonable deed that deserves such punishment? What such act are they about to commit or could we possibly commit?

Wanting to know God's revelation on all subjects and desiring to be informed on every theme, we begin to listen to the harsh but helpful words of the passage before us. Let every ear listen. Let every foot walk the path of life and avoid the trail of death.

THE UNFATHOMABLE LOVE OF GOD

God's unfathomable love is the theme of all Scripture. It is the message of the entire book of Hebrews. The opening chapter of the epistle began, "God, having of old time spoken unto the fathers in the prophets."

That is an evidence of the love of God.

Can you imagine that the Creator of the galaxies would condescend to communicate with dwellers on this speck of dust called earth? Yet God has revealed to men His will. He has spoken to us through prophets. He has brought His commandments for humanity through angels. Most importantly, He has shown His nature and His gospel through His own Son. A small grasp of astronomy shouts of the condescension of our Maker. The vastness of space is nothing compared to the immensity of God's love for his creatures. It is unfathomable that God would love the world to the degree that He would communicate at all, especially communicate in person. The burden of chapters 1 and 2 of Hebrews is that love led God to speak through prophets and angels and now through the Son.

Chapters 3 and 4 declare that God's unfathomable love went beyond words and included deliverance. History recalled God stepping into time and space to deliver Israel in the days of Moses and Joshua. The gospel proclaimed the intervention of God in Jesus to bring salvation from sin. Old Testament records spoke of the exodus and the guiding pillar of fire and protective cloud that brought Israel from Egypt to the Promised Land. New Testament writings reveal deliverance from Satanic bondage and Christ's leadership of his people all the way to heaven itself. What unfathomable love.

In Chapters 5, 6, and 7 comes the assurance that our amazing God handles for His people the problem of sin. Here we meet priests and sacrifices for sin. Here we are pointed to Jesus as the "better" priest and the "better" sacrifice. Again God's unfathomable love has brought us

Christ the High Priest, who offers "mercy, and grace to help us in time of need" (4:16). Then chapters 8, 9, and 10 expound the covenant that is ours because of God's unfathomable love. That new covenant, foreshadowed in the old, brings life everlasting and joy in God's presence forever. All these bounties belong to those who keep that covenant which was sealed by the blood of Christ.

No one can read the first ten chapters of Hebrews without sensing the unfathomable love of God. No heart can but want to sing the inquiry of Robert Harkness, "Why should He love me so? Why should my Savior to Calvary go? Why should He love me so?"[1] The hymn writer raises the question verse after verse, chorus after chorus. But he never dreams of answering it, because the love of God is beyond our comprehension. As another poet wrote:

> The wonder of wonders is not to me that Jesus created the sun to rule by day and pursue its way and its trackless journey to run.
> The wonder of wonders is to me that God should for one moment potentially see and empty His veins of love divine that I His child might be.
> The wonder of wonders is not to me that Jesus created a star and a stellular world create and make free to illumine earth and worlds afar.
> To be sure that is a wonder, a wonder sublime, but a greater wonder is to me that Jesus should die on Calvary. Die just for love's sake and undertake out of a sinner like me to make a being to outshine the sun as it forever its journey may run. That is a mystery, a wonder to me. Enable us Lord to glorify thee.[2]

What unfathomable love!

THE UNPARDONABLE SIN OF MAN

We ever need to remind ourselves of the love of God. That is the teaching of the Bible. We must also hear another truth in the same inspired book. Hebrews 10 unfolds the possibility of some readers endangering their souls by the unpardonable sin.

We need to ask again what sin is, what it does and what it demands. But we must inquire also the nature of this particular sin which is said to be without pardon.

Bible passages in every direction speak of God's willingness to forgive penitent sinners. If a woman taken in the very act of adultery is offered hope and a thief on a cross can be assured of Paradise, what sin can be beyond pardon? Noah, who got drunk, Saul of Tarsus, who saw to the murder of many believers, and tax collectors, who had been dishonest, all meet the offer of God's forgiveness. What sin can be so horrible in the light of God's unfathomable love, that it is beyond forgiveness?

Any sin separates a man from God. All sin demands such an atonement that the requirements of both God's love and His justice are met. There are sins of omission and sins of commission. Some sin by rebelling against the instruction of the Lord. They leave undone His commands. Others choose to go where God forbids and to act when God says, "Thou shalt not." Sin is rebellion against God. It is pitting the corrupt human will against the perfect divine will. All sin separates. Christ's blood can cleanse from all sin. What is this one exception? What is this particular sin that is said to be unpardonable?

The writer of Hebrews begins the paragraph before

us with the words, "For if we sin willfully" (10:26). He does not say "they" or "you," but "we." The author is not talking here about non-believers. He is addressing Christians. His warning includes both the readers of the epistle and its writer. He writes, "if we sin willfully after that we have received the knowledge of the truth, there remaineth no more a sacrifice for sins." We must conclude that this sin beyond pardon is a possibility not only in the world, but, also in the church. The "we" of the sentence shows that a real danger exists not alone for believers but even for Bible writers such as the author of Hebrews himself.

It is informative to note that this dreadful deed is done "willfully" and not accidentally. When this sin is committed, it is done on purpose. It is done "after that we have received the knowledge of the truth." Without exhausting the subject, we at least should note that this sin has to do with setting "at naught" (10:28) revelation from God, treading "under foot the Son of God," counting "the blood of the covenant . . . an unholy thing" and doing "despite unto the Spirit of grace" (10:29).

In the Sermon on the Mount Jesus considered salt that had lost its savor as being "good for nothing, but to be . . . trodden under foot" (Matt. 5:13). A person treads under foot that which is of no importance to him whatsoever. The people described by the Hebrews' author are apostatizing from the church. They are rejecting the Holy Spirit's gracious call. They are reckoning of no importance the Messiah, his gospel and his blood-purchased covenant. I assure you that backsliding is bad. Sin of every stripe is evil. Disobedience is never right. But one thing is worse. To finally and totally turn one's back on God's offer of salvation by grace is the sin of all sins. It is the complete rejection of "the sacrifice for sins" offered by Jesus. The refusal of his sacrifice leaves no others. "There remaineth" no other "sacrifice" that can remove sin's condemnation. The unfathomable love of God offered salvation to all. The unpardonable sin of man would be to reject finally and completely that proffered forgiveness.

THE UNQUENCHABLE FIRE OF HELL

God's love refused with finality is the only sin that places a person beyond hope. The opposite of the joys of the redeemed in glory is the anguish of the lost in Gehenna. The text before us speaks of "fearful expectation" and of "fierceness of fire." It tells of a "sorer punishment" than known in Israel's experience with broken law. It promises a "vengeance." It calls it "a fearful thing to fall into the hands of the living God" (10:27-31).

Such a hell is, is future, is certain and is unquenchable. Jesus is the one that taught his followers about hell. Their Old Testaments gave but scant information. It was the Master Teacher who, having magnified the love of God, also revealed the realities of future existence apart from Him. His teaching contained the good news that "He that believeth and is baptized shall be saved." It also brought the bad news that "he that disbelieveth shall be condemned," or damned (Mark 16:16). John 3:16-17 held out the glorious truth of God's love for the world, which sent Jesus not to judge any but to save all. Yet the same book and chapter at a later verse lifted up the needed warning that eternal life is for believers, but the abiding wrath of God is upon all who "obey not the Son" (John 3:36). In the light of Jesus' words, we must agree that hell is, and hell is awful. Explaining to his disciples what eternal separation from God would be like, Jesus made some comparisons. He taught hell to be like fire, for his followers knew the pain and horror of being burned. He spoke of hell as a bottomless pit. To dream of falling and falling throughout eternity in a pit without a bottom brought the awareness of how awful it would be to be forever separated from God and all that is good. One day Jesus termed hell outer-darkness. Anyone who had been in a situation of total blackness, where the next step might lead to unknown tragedy, recognized the warning in Jesus' appeal to avoid hell at all cost. To be where you know not what lies ahead, behind or on either side is frightening at the very thought. What is over your head or under your feet is unknown to one in a darkness that is total. The word "gehenna," that Jesus used for hell, called to mind Jerusalem's garbage dump. All the figures he used to describe life without God cried out that hell was dreadful and to be shunned.

If it were but momentary, or but for a short while, perhaps the strongest would survive it and go on. But the Lord called hell eternal. No wonder Hebrews 10:31 calls it "a fearful thing to fall into the hands of the living God." Let no reader fail to hear the options spoken by the prophet Habakkuk. The righteous "shall live by faith." If one "shrink back" God will say, "My soul hath no pleasure in him" (Heb. 10:38). The encouraging line that ends this chapter is that "We are not of them that shrink back unto perdition; but of them that have faith unto the saving of the soul" (10:9). The destruction of the soul is not God's desire. Rather, it is the saving of that soul. We will either know pardon or we will know perdition. We will either keep on marching toward the Holy City of heaven with God's people or we will draw back to the loss of our salvation. We, in the words of John the Baptist, will either be baptized by Christ in the Holy Spirit, experiencing every joy in the garner of heaven, or we will be immersed by him in the "unquenchable fire" awaiting the lost (cp. Matt. 3:7-12). From this there is no escape, for a great gulf has been fixed. There is no passing after death from one state to the other.

THE UNREASONABLE DEED OF REJECTION

Analyzing the love of God, we learn how unfathomable it is. Recognizing the unpardonable sin, we see how destructive it is, for it leads to the unquenchable fire where in the future the unforgiven shall go forever. We now must study to find what is this unreasonable deed that is the act beyond pardon.

Think of four "C's," Cross, Christ, Covenant and Comforter. These four are suggested in the passage we are attempting to understand. It reads, "There remaineth no more sacrifice for sins" (10:26). The effectual sacrifice for sins was the death of Christ on the cross of Calvary. The church rightly sings, "There's no other way but this; I shall ne're get sight of the Gates of Light, If the way of the cross I miss."[1] The author of Hebrews has shown that animal sacrifice accomplished nothing in removing sin, but that Jesus' death brought total cleansing to all who believe in his atoning death. To turn one's back upon Jesus' "sacrifice for sins," leaves no other saving sacrifice.

Move to the next "C," Christ. On the old rugged cross was shed not just blood, it was the blood of "the Son of God." To reject the Christ left no other Saviour. He is the only Son of God, the only Saviour. There is no one else remaining in heaven to later come incarnate and die for the world's sins. There neither is nor can be another.

"Covenant" is the word that now catches our eye in verse 29. God has made a new covenant in Christ's blood. That contract will stand forever. To reject it and look for another would be to move from solid, enduring rock to sand that certainly will sink beneath our feet. The old covenant was temporal but the new covenant is to last forever. The book of Hebrews will close with a benediction that refers to "the blood of an eternal covenant" (13:20).

"Comforter" is not a word found in verse 29, but the phrase "the Spirit of grace" is found there. The lost are said to be those who have "done despite unto the Spirit of grace." The Holy Spirit, the gracious Spirit of God, pleads with men to accept Christ and remain in covenant with God's Son. When we reject this heavenly calling, or continually renounce this Holy One who calls, we find we have sinned against no less than the Holy Spirit of God himself. God will forgive every other sin. No matter what has been done or said, it can be forgiven and forgotten by the salvation purchased at Calvary. But to constantly say no to the undeserved offer and ever to turn the back toward the offerer's outstretched arms, leaves but the option of getting the justly deserved consequence of our foolish choice.

Love brought Calvary. But love cannot save those who reject the way of the cross. Love cannot rescue anyone who refuses to be in the covenant that promises forgiveness. The dreadful Scripture before us is important to hear, for it makes clear our condition. After all that God has done to bring salvation to us, He cannot rescue one person that refuses the offered nail-pierced hand of Jesus. Let God's grace and not God's wrath be your choice.

Endnotes

1. "Why Should He Love Me So?" *Hymns for the Family of God* (Nashville, Tenn: Paragon Associates, Inc., 1976), p. 26.
2. Author unknown.
3. Jessie B. Pounds, "The Way of the Cross Leads Home" *Favorite Hymns of Praise* (Wheaton, IL: Tabernacle Pub. Co., 1967), p. 402. Copyright Rodeheaver Co.

PART FIVE

Jesus, the Appealer to Man's Purest Motives

CHAPTER EIGHTEEN

Audio-Visual Faith
Hebrews 11:1-40

(The Appeal of Faith)

Remember the signs you see at Railroad Crossings? They call on all to "Stop, Look and Listen." As we deal with Biblical faith as described in Hebrews 11, we need to stop and look, because faith is visible. We ought to stop and listen, in that faith is audible. Genuine faith, as taught in Scripture, is audio-visual.

The preceding chapter of Hebrews concluded by announcing that Christians "live by faith" (verse 38) and that they "have faith unto the saving of the soul" (verse 39). The present chapter amplifies what that life of faith implies. When a person falls in love, he finds it difficult not to let it show. A sparkle will be in the eye and words will slip through the lips. Love and faith are very much alike. Lovers and believers can not keep their love and faith quiet. They will talk about it. It will be visible in the way they act.

With Hebrews 11 open before our eyes, notice what

the author has placed there. He has begun with the opening pages of his Old Testament. He pulls examples of faith from Genesis and Exodus. He finds illustrations from the book of Joshua to those of Samuel and Kings. His entire Bible serves as a picture book of heroes who walked by faith. They kept believing through adversity. They would not turn back. They continued in their faith to the day they died. Now let the readers, who have come to faith in Christ, not turn back. This chapter of Hebrews 11 demonstrates that a Christian returning to Judaism was turning *from* the Old Testament heroes. He was not turning *to* them. The forty verses in the passage define what faith is and what faith does.

Let us ask these two basic questions: "What is faith?" and "What does faith do?" In response to the first question let us learn from six men, some recent, some ancient. As to the second investigation let us select six examples from the many cases presented in our text.

WHAT FAITH IS

Alexander Campbell

The nineteenth century reformer, Alexander Campbell, spoke of faith as the belief of testimony. To him faith was always preceded by fact and followed by feeling. I might believe that a loved-one had been hurt. It may not be true. Yet, if I believe it, I will feel very sad. The feeling follows what I believe. Should I rather think that something wonderful had happened to one dear to me, the consequence will be a feeling of joy. There always will be feeling following faith. But whether that feeling is justified depends upon the fact that precedes the faith. Was the fact dependable? Was it worthy of my trust?

I believe Mr. Campbell was right. First of all there was the fact of Jesus' death, burial and resurrection. The apostles, who witnessed Christ alive, proclaimed what they had seen and heard. Those who believed their testimony found a joyous feeling bubbling up from deep within them. First was the fact. Next was the faith. Following was the feeling.

What is most important is that in which you put your faith. Do not put too much faith in your faith. It is not the greatness of your faith that saves. It is the greatness of the Christ in whom you place your faith. In the Garden of Eden the tempter spoke to Eve. She believed his lie, acted upon it and it led to her condemnation. Her believing is not the important part of the story. It is that in which she foolishly placed her confidence. We must place our trust in God himself, for He alone is worthy.

Visualize yourself walking across a plank that spans a stream. You had enough faith in the strength of the board to begin your walk. You will get safely to the other side, if the timber in which you put your trust does not fail you. Should the plank have been rotten, it will matter not how much faith you had. In that instance this plank would break under your weight and into the water you would go. There needs to be a solid fact upon which to build your faith. Following that faith will be the feeling of confident joy.

Martin Luther

Martin Luther, the Anglo-Saxon priest that launched

the Protestant reformation in the sixteenth century, understood New Testament faith to be trust. The Greek word (πίστις), he translated into Latin as *fiducia*, rather than *fides*. *Fides* was belief in the sense of mentally assenting to a creedal statement. *Fiducia*, on the other hand, was belief in the sense of putting one's trust in a person. Romans was Paul's epistle calling for trust in Jesus as God's Son and the Justifier of men.

James, the half-brother of Jesus, makes this distinction. He declares that the demons of hell believe "that God is one" (James 2:19). To mentally agree with the Bible's assertions about God, or even with the historical facts of Jesus' life and resurrection, is not soul-saving. But, faith in the deeper sense of placing one's very life in Christ's care justifies.

Rudolph Bultmann

Campbell's insights regarding faith are helpful. Luther's emphasis on the subject is informative. Even the more recent Theologian Rudolph Bultmann has something constructive to add. From his existentialist perspective, he sees faith grasping one's entire being. Believing has not alone to do with the mind.

Entscheidung was a useful German word to Bultmann. God called for radical decision on man's part. Each person by the gospel was called to throw his entire life, his whole being, into the arms of God. When such a total surrender is God's demand, faith is no less than complete obedience. Let no one talk about believing who is not submitting his will to Christ's will or who is not acting as Jesus commands.

Dwight L. Moody

Campbell, Luther and Bultmann have spoken on the topic of faith. Before we listen to Luke and then the author of Hebrews, give ear to the late evangelist Dwight L. Moody. To him our question has to do with the source of faith. Where does it come from?

Moody's response runs something like this. "I used to pray and pray and pray for faith. Then I read Romans 10:17 that 'belief cometh of hearing, and hearing by the word of Christ.' So I stopped praying and started reading." Paul taught that faith comes by hearing God's word. There is virtue in praying, but intercession alone over many years can not by itself produce trust. What builds faith is hearing God's promises and becoming aware of God's nature and learning of His faithfulness to all with whom He made covenant in the past. Even more important than talking to God is listening to God. In the Scriptures there is proof regarding His Son. Evidence of Jesus' resurrection, fulfillment in Christ of the old prophecies, and instance after instance of unmerited love expressed to people — this is what builds faith.

Luke

Luke, the physician who traveled with Paul, is the author of both his Gospel and his book of Acts. It is good to address our question about faith to him. The last lines of his Gospel recall Christ's orders for "repentance and remission of sins . . . (to) be preached . . . unto all the nations" (Luke 24:47). The entire book of Acts tells of that proclamation bringing faith wherever it was heralded from Jerusalem "unto the uttermost part of the earth" (Acts 1:8).

Province after province and city after city gave witness to the fact that wherever the message was preached faith was born. It is a truism that after the gospel event came the proclamation of that event and after the preaching came the believing. First is the fact. Following is the proclamation. Next comes the faith that is followed by obedience. In every case of conversion in Acts the order of events is the same. Listeners heard the story, believed it and were "baptized in the name of Jesus Christ unto the remission of . . . sins" (Acts 2:38). To Luke faith roots in the Word and fruits in obedience.

Hebrews
With open Bibles at Hebrews 11, we want to see how faith is spoken of here. The chapter begins, "Now faith is assurance of things hoped for, a conviction of things not seen" (11:1). In other words, faith is the attitude of total trust. Believers walk in the assurance and conviction that God does not lie. One always can believe His word. Whatever He says about the past or the future is to be trusted.

The past is already past. One either believes or disbelieves the opening lines of Genesis about creation or early history. There is no way to place those happenings in a test-tube and relive them today. The past cannot be "seen," but believers trust the written testimony.

The future is still future. You are not in heaven at this moment establishing by sight the reality of the Holy City. As the past is long gone and the future is yet to come, both are now relegated to the realm of faith. What we have about yesterday and tomorrow is the Word of God. It brings "assurance of things hoped for" in the future. It produces "conviction of things not seen" in days gone by or in places beyond view.

At this very moment Christians believe that Jesus is at the Father's right hand and is interceding for them. We cannot see him with our physical eyes for he is beyond the veil. Yet we doubt not his present ministry on our behalf, for we have his word and it is trustworthy. With eyes of faith we can see him who is invisible and believe that he can do the impossible. The word of God has produced that confidence.

WHAT FAITH DOES

To the Hebrews' author faith is believing all that God says. It is also doing everything that God asks. To the writer faith has a root. All faith is rooted in God's declaration. It also bears a fruit. Biblical faith ever produces an action. That is why we are asserting faith to be audio-visual. It does not remain internal. It expresses itself in a deed.

Quite often God places before us a test of faith. Something that appears to be illogical is asked to see if we really trust Him. Remember the exodus story where Israelites were told to sacrifice a lamb. They were assured that, when this blood was applied to doorpost and lintel, the death angel would pass over the home and the first born would be saved from death. Logically speaking there existed no scientific evidence that lamb blood on doors would divert death. Yet they took God at his word. They did what He said. Their obedience was an act of faith.

When Naaman the Syrian was told to dip seven times

in the muddy Jordan and his leprosy would disappear, no man in history had ever been cured from the dread disease in this manner before. Evidence from some lab was not produced to prove a direct connection between dirty water and healing. Naaman had only the prophet's word from God. He obeyed. He was healed. He had passed the test of faith.

Joshua was ordered to march around Jericho seven days and seven times on the seventh day. He was promised that the city walls would collapse at the blowing of the trumpets. That was a test of faith. No invader had proven by similar actions before that protective walls fall this way. The order from God might appear to be in error. Joshua evidenced his trust in God by unquestionable obedience.

As members of the church, consider the water of baptism. Can any relationship be proved rationally between this ordinance and the removal of sin? How could God's servant Ananias hold a straight face when he tells Saul of Tarsus, "Arise, and be baptized, and wash away thy sins" (Acts 22:16)? What possible connection can there be between physical burial of a body in water and the guilty heart of a man being cleansed? Learn from the many examples of Hebrews 11. Believers never question authority. Believers believe everything God says. They will not be deterred by rationalistic doubts. If God said it, they do it and that settles it.

Faith always expresses itself. Faith ever responds to the will of God declared. Faith is always doing things. It cannot be kept quiet. It acts. Faith gets feet to marching. Faith gets hands to building. Faith sets hearts to hoping. Faith makes walls of separation fall down.

Abel

Look at just a few of the many examples our author provides. Abel heads the list. Verse 4 begins, "By faith Abel offered unto God a more excellent sacrifice than Cain." Your earlier study of prior chapters in Hebrews found only two uses of the word faith. Now you have come to a single chapter that has the word twenty times. You read "by faith," "by faith," "by faith." Each Old Testament character hears a command from God and does what is commanded. Though the ancient Bible stories did not use the word faith, the Hebrew writer calls each instance by that term.

Abel, like his brother Cain, was told to bring a sacrifice. For Abel's sacrifice to be "by faith," it had to be specified by God. Cain's offering did not please God, for he rationalized that a sacrifice from the field in which he worked ought to be as acceptable as one from a flock. If God asked for a blood sacrifice, would not a gift of equal value do, since Cain, after all, did not raise sheep? The old proverb suggests the answer, "You can not squeeze blood out of a turnip." When God has spoken, either obedience or rebellion are the options. God is not looking for rational excuses. He is pleased by unhesitating obedience.

Noah

"By faith Noah being warned of God . . . prepared an ark" (v. 7). Whoever had seen rains fall and streams rise to flood the entire earth, as Noah had been informed would be the case with his world? He began preaching, for he believed God's word to him. He started building the boat in spite of the ridicule, because he believed what he was told. His faith, like all genuine faith, is audio-visual. Watch him work. Listen to him preach. You know he has faith. It is obvious.

Abraham
"By faith Abraham, when he was called, obeyed" (v. 8). He had never "seen" the Promised Land. But he left Ur of the Chaldees, by faith. He traveled as a sojourner with only the promise of a land. All his actions give evidence that he is a believer in God's promises.

Christians are just like Abraham. Their faith is in the unseen. They believe all the Old Testament from the Creation story to the writing of Malachi. Yet their eyes did not see even one of the historical happenings that are there recorded. They have confidence in every New Testament event. They profess Jesus' virgin birth, sinless life, atoning death and glorious resurrection but are personal witnesses to none of the items they confess. Faith is the belief of testimony. Actions evidence where faith is.

Moses and Joshua
Moses had Egyptian armies to the rear. He had mountains on one side. Ahead was the sea. God ordered him to lead the children of Israel through the Red Sea (v. 29). When God called for the people to march, he expected obedience. They started marching and the water began to part forming walls on either side.

Once again faith is seen to root in God's word and to fruit in man's obedience. It is the same in the case of Joshua. The city of Jericho was enemy ground. God's people received word as to His instruction. Strange as were the orders, they acted promptly, obediently and as specified. "By faith the walls of Jericho fell down" (v. 30) are the words written about the victory. They were winners because God told them what to do and they did what they were told.

Martyrs

Hebrews 11 lists as heroes of faith some we might consider losers. The chapter does not only tell of subdued kingdoms and stopped lions' mouths because of faith, it records the stories of people dying for their faith. It tells of people who "were tortured . . . stoned . . . sawn asunder . . . slain with the sword . . . destitute, afflicted, ill treated" (vv. 35-38). They too walked by faith.

This writer is averring that not every Old Testament character received what was promised in this world. But they kept right on. They did not stop trusting God. "These all, having witness borne to them through their faith, received not the promise, God having provided for them some better thing concerning us, that apart from us they should not be made perfect" (vv. 39-40).

In the roll of heroes stand the names of believers. These are they that hear the words of God, do what He says and are numbered with the conquerors. Christ ever appeals to mankind's holiest, highest and purest qualities. He never lures his hearers to hollow ground but to heavenly values. Calling for faith in God is the appeal to one of man's purest motives.

CHAPTER NINETEEN

"Amen! Ouch!"
Hebrews 12:1-13

(The Appeal to Courage)

After reading most Bible verses, the hearts of believers say, "Amen!" The more appropriate response in some cases would be "Ouch!!" As we learn what God has done for His people and how Christ has died for our sins, the ready "Amen!" is the accurate expression of deep appreciation. But when we learn from Scripture that hardships and difficulties are to be expected in the lives of Jesus' followers, we are quick to say, "Ouch!"

What is our task in the church? Is it demanding? Is it difficult? Does "Ouch" really fit? Hebrews 12:1-13 pictures believers as running a race. Is running to win ever easy? Jesus, it is said, "endured the cross" (12:2). There was nothing easy about Calvary. Some of the recipients of the Hebrews epistle found that their hands did "hang down" and they had "palsied knees" (12:12). All runners have had times when lifting their leaden legs seemed more than they could do. At the beginning of the Christian race, it may have seemed easy. Now at the end of many laps, continuing to press ahead appears impossible. It would be easier to turn "out of the way," or to get off the track, than to follow the instruction to hold to "straight paths for your feet" (12:13). Life is hard. Staying at it is difficult.

Whoever wrote Hebrews thought of the Christian life in athletic terms, much as did Paul. The apostle to the Gentiles compared living for Christ to boxing. Every blow must count, for shadow-boxing is not a real battle. Our fight is not imaginary. Therefore he wrote, "So fight I, as not beating the air" (I Cor. 9:26). To the Philippians his comparison was to running in a race, where runners stretch every muscle to reach the finish line first, so they will not be losers. His words were, "Forgetting the things which are behind, and stretching forward to the things which are before, I press on toward the goal unto the prize of the high calling of God in Christ Jesus (Phil. 3:13-14). Turning to wrestling, Paul knew life in the church to demand all-out exertion. In that day it was not simply a matter of pinning the opponents shoulders to a mat. They fought for life itself. One combatant did not live. So to the Ephesians Paul reminded that "our wrestling is not against flesh and blood, but against the principalities, against the powers, against the world rulers of this darkness, against the spiritual hosts of wickedness in the heavenly places" (Eph. 6:12).

What Paul says to his readers, our author writes to the Hebrews. They must win. They dare not lose. Let them know that the Christian life is demanding. There is suffering in it. While we rejoice in hearing of Jesus' agonizing for us, we need to know the fact that there may be hardships along the way for you and me. In a race it is not just a short sprint or momentary support that brings the grandstanders to cheer. What matters in the end is whether you have that dogged stick-to-itiveness that keeps you in the race through the last lap. That is essential to win.

The practical message for you and me in Hebrews 12 is three-fold. To each Christian the grandstand is important. Rooters cheering one on have a significant place in victory. Likewise, the goal is vital. Why all the preparations and struggles to win, if in the end the prize is not worth it? Grit and gumption stand third. No athlete bypasses the push-ups, the jogging or the practice and still wins. Hard things must be done by every one who plans on winning.

THE GRANDSTAND

The first verse of our text begins:

> Therefore let us also, seeing that we are compassed about with so great a cloud of witnesses, lay aside every weight, and the sin which doth so easily beset us, and let us run with patience the race that is set before us, looking unto Jesus the author and perfecter of our faith, who for the joy that was set before him endured the cross, despising shame, and hath sat down at the right hand of the throne of God (Heb. 12:1-2).

The previous chapter (11) listed Old Testament heroes. In each case it was pointed out that their accomplishments were "by faith." The point of the author was that each saint of old lived in faith up to his death.

Recall that the record reads, "By faith Jacob, when he was dying" did thus and so (11:21). "By faith, Joseph, when his end was nigh" acted as he did (11:22). Listing many who met death by faith, the author concludes, "And these all, having had witness borne to them through their faith, received not the promise, God having provided some better thing concerning us, that apart from us they should not be made perfect" (11:39-40). The lesson the reader is to gain from this is that the heroes are heroes not just because they heard the word of God and started, but because they heard the word of God and just would not give up. They remained faithful to the very point of their death. Let anyone wanting to be like an Old Testament hero, keep in the race until he or she breaks the tape at the end of the course.

"We are compassed about with so great a cloud of witnesses," says the passage. This refers to the grandstand filled with people that cheer you on, wanting you to win. That list of supporters includes all whose names are written in the preceding chapter. You know that the slate would include all past and present New Testament saints as well.

My plea to you is not only to realize how many supporters you have, but also to recruit you to cheer others to keep on running. Some brothers or sisters will flag in zeal, or get discouraged and throw in the towel, if some word of encouragement does not revive their spirits. Get to cheering. Root them on. Don't allow them to fail in the game. Your note in writing, your encouraging visit or your phone call to say you care, will turn them into victors.

The first quarter of the basketball game in the playoffs is demanding. But it is nothing compared with the last minutes of the final quarter. No player dare let down no matter how tired he becomes. The coach may call a brief time-out so by his words he can re-charge his team into champions. A factor that makes the difference between winning or losing is the grandstand. Their cheers, like a shot of adrenalin, puts extra power into the players.

God needs you in His cheering section. Just to cry out, "Hold that line" or "Block that kick" can make a difference in a football game. To shout, "Yea team, Let's go" adds to the possibility of victory in any sport. Usually in church the words are rather "Amen," "Praise the Lord" or "Hallelujah." These sanctified shouts are worshipers' ways of encouraging their comrades that Christ is leading to victory and all of us should stay on the winning team.

Is it ever right in a worship service to clap? Opinions may differ here. Many think that when some believer is singing a solo, reading a Scripture, bearing a testimony or playing a favorite hymn on some instrument, it is appropriate for the others to say by applause, "We are with you. We are behind you. We are glad that you are using your talents in the service of God." To these Christians, clapping is a form of "amen" showing agreement with the message given.

Some even understand history to tell of believers being thrown to lions in the first century. On those occasions the temptation to renounce Christ, and thus escape being the next prisoner to die in this horrible way, was real temptation. By applauding, the Christians gave the next in line the strength of heart to go on at every cost.

Be an encourager. Grandstands, cheering sections, encouragers are the need of the hour. Many are the temptations to turn aside and quit. Encouragement may be your ministry. Every town, every church, every individual needs such a ministry. Shepherding the local flock so none stray from the fold is a major responsibility. However well done or poorly done is the ministry of encouragement in your congregation, you are also needed to supplement that ministry. Let fellow members know you are in their rooting section. Assure them that you are going to continue encouraging them until the game is over. Thank God for the grandstand full of believers that give cheering words that spur God's people on.

THE GOAL

"We are compassed about with so great a cloud of witnesses." We do need to "lay aside every weight and the sin which doth so easily beset us." That encumbrance that holds us back is discouragement. "Let us run with patience," or steadfastness, or perseverance, "the race that is set before us, looking unto Jesus the author and perfector of our faith." Now the writer of Hebrews is pointing to the goal.

Christ is the starting line of the Christian religion. He is also the final tape toward whom we run as goal. The reason for all the struggles of preparation and the hardships of the course is to one day be Christlike. Jesus is the "author," or the one who started us on the way. He is the one we are to keep our eyes upon. We hear the cheers of the grandstand but we do not look aside toward them. The winner keeps his eyes ahead toward the goal. To be like Jesus is his single aim.

The hymn is accurate. We sing the question of Thomas Shepherd, "Must Jesus bear the cross alone, And all the world go free?" We continue the answer, "No; there's a cross for ev'ry one, And there's a cross for me."[1] When I look at the Christ of the cross, I learn how to face hardship.

Peter reminded the church under government opposition that "Christ also suffered for you, leaving you an example, that ye should follow his steps" (I Pet. 2:21). Those who follow in the steps of the Saviour are to expect some of the wrath that came against their Master. His way, and thus our way, is not to be easy. But each hardship faced is easier to bear, when we look to Jesus who showed us how to suffer. Our example has gone before us, so thumbs up Christians. Keep on.

It was "for the joy that was set before him" that Christ "endured the cross" (Heb. 12:2). What joy? The joy of bringing redeemed men and women to his Father. The agony of the cross became worth it, for the end in view was mankind's salvation. He despised the shame of a world booing him. His own nation cried out, "Crucify him." Yet he endured the agony and despised the reproach for accomplishing human salvation. Thus he now "hath sat down at the right hand of the throne of God." We, too, can face ridicule and suffering when we remember why we are in the race and what prize lies before us. We, too, are spending our energies in winning the world. We, too, will be crowned with the honor of abiding eternally with Jesus. Whatever price we must pay will be worth it, for ahead of us at the end of the race is being like Christ.

THE GRIT

What is this quality that the writer of Hebrews is urging on his readers? What is this character, or nature, that a Christ-like person has? "Grit" is one word that describes a Jesus-like person. Each follower of God's Son must reflect perseverance. Every athlete knows he must stay at it. When every joint aches and each muscle is sore, he keeps on. There must, in the nature of the sport, be practice and exertion to the point of exhaustion. With pains in the legs and the chest, you dare not stop. Only the one who gives his utmost can expect to win. So it is with Christianity.

Cartoons in the paper and programs on T.V. have introduced us to Ma and Pa Kettle. One recurring thought is, "If you want me, you must take my whole family." The clear line running through the New Testament is, "If you want Christ, you must take what goes along with the Christian religion."

Hardship is joined to the Saviour. The symbol of the church for the centuries has been the cross. It is said that of the 318 who gathered at the Council of Nicea, only twelve were unscarred. Have you ever tried to climb a cliff overlooking the beach or to scale a steep mountainside? If the hill were smooth you would slip and fall to the bottom. The rough craigs and extended boulders provided you with something on which to ascend upward. Difficulties are the bumps on which to climb to glory.

"Press on! Surmount the rocky steeps. Climb boldly oe'r the torrent's arch. He fails alone who feebly creeps. He wins who dares the hero's march."[2]

Endnotes

1. "Must Jesus Bear the Cross Alone?" *Favorite Hymns of Praise* (Wheaton, IL: Tabernacle Publishing Co., 1967), p. 189.
2. Author unknown.

CHAPTER TWENTY

Choosing Mountains
Hebrews 12:14-29

(The Appeal to Decision)

Fellow travelers, it is time to make a choice. The trail divides and no person can follow both paths at the same time. If selection of the road for our life to follow were only a decision between good and evil, the choice could be more easily made.

The poet John Oxenham wrote:

> "To every man there openeth A Way, and Ways, and a way. And the High Soul climbs the High Way, and the Low Soul gropes the Low, And in between, on the misty flats, The rest drift to and fro. But to every man there openeth A High Way and a Low, every man decideth The Way his soul shall go.[1]

The choice the author of Hebrews places before his readers is more than the option between righteousness and inquity. It is more specifically the decision between the way of human works or the way of divine grace, as the road that leads to heaven. As the writer of our epistle has built over many chapters his case for staying with Christianity rather than reverting to Judaism, he now clearly lays out the alternatives. He appeals for each reader to be "looking carefully lest there be any man that falleth short of (or, falleth back from) the grace of God" (Heb. 12:15). He warns how the wrong choice of a moment can have unchanging consequences. Esau, he reminds us, "for one mess of meat sold his birthright" (12:16). The damage was irrevokable.

Let those considering leaving Christ be aware of the end of such a trail. The road of good-works and the keeping of Moses' law, because of human frailty, leads to judgment. The road of God's unmerited favor toward sinners leads to justification. To trust in one's own goodness will not save. To rely on God's goodness is redemptive for all.

Verses 18-21 reveal the trail that leads up Mount Sinai. Verses 22-29 show the path that leads to Mount Zion. The way of Sinai is the way of demands, the way of darkness and the way of death. Let the Israelites recall the giving of the ten commandments (cp. Exod. 19). The mountain "burned with fire." There was "blackness, and darkness, and tempest" (18). The people "could not endure that which was enjoined" (20). It was "so fearful . . . that Moses said, I exceedingly fear and quake" (21). To opt for Sinai is to opt for death. Even one law broken and condemnation awaits the violator.

The good news of Jesus, the new covenant, is a different road. Grace leads to life. The way of holiness that Christ offers has only blessings and no curses *en route* and at the end. Seven good fruits are listed to help readers choose the gospel way.

THE HOLY CITY

"But ye are come unto mount Zion, and unto the city of the living God, the heavenly Jerusalem" (13:22). Israel's earthly capital, Jerusalem, was soon to be lost to their foes. But, Christians could not be losers, for they were citizens of a city no Roman military force could surround and topple. Each believer who had opted for Christ could say, "Our citizenship is in heaven; whence also we wait for a Saviour, the Lord Jesus Christ" (Phil.3:20). The Palestinian capital could be captured, "But the Jerusalem that is above is free, which is our mother" (Gal. 4:26).

How wise was Abraham who "looked for the city which hath foundations, whose builder and maker is God" (Heb. 11:10). The true sons of Abraham have received "a kingdom that cannot be shaken" (Heb. 12:28). Such could not have been said of magnificent Babylon. It was shaken to its foundations by Medo-Persia, as Medo-Persia collapsed later under Alexander the Great and Alexander's Greece still later fell before mighty Rome. History is the record of the rise and fall of nations. Prophecy, such as Daniel 2, is that history written before it happened. The book of Revelation foresaw the collapse of Rome, that was erringly being called eternal Rome. Jesus' apocalyptic discourse of Matthew 24 foretold the desolation of Jerusalem and its temple. How much more secure is the church against which "the gates of Hades shall not prevail" (Matt. 16:18).

THE HOLY ANGELS

To come to Christ was to "come unto mount

Zion . . . the heavenly Jerusalem." It was also to come "to innumerable hosts of angels" (12:22). These myriads of angels number "ten thousand times ten thousand, and thousands and thousands" (Rev. 5:11). These angelic beings are interested in our salvation. They rejoice at even one sinner's conversion to Christ. They are commissioned "to do service for the sake of them that shall inherit salvation" (Heb. 1:14). They will accompany the Lord to earth when he comes to judge the world. Until that day they act as guardians of those who by faith choose the mount of grace over the mount of law.

THE HOLY CHURCH

To spur the correct decision to remain with Christ, the list of benefits extends. There goes with the proper choice, not only "the city of the living God . . . and . . . innumerable hosts of angels," there is "the general assembly and church of the firstborn who are enrolled in heaven" (12:23).

This festal assembly is the church composed of firstborn ones (the Greek is plural). As the firstborn was the heir, all in the church are in on the inheritance as firstborn ones.

All individuals at their acceptance of Jesus Christ are in one Spirit . . . baptized into one body, whether Jews or Greek, whether bond or free, and . . . made to drink of one Spirit" (I Cor. 12:13). Each believer is part of the "one, holy, apostolic and catholic church," to use the phrase of ancient creeds.

The King James Version of Acts 2:47 tells that "the Lord added to the church daily such as should be saved." To be united to Christ was to be joined to his body. To belong to the church of God was to be part of "an elect race, a royal priesthood, a holy nation, a people for God's own possession" (I Pet. 2:9).

Our basis of joy, as members of Christ's church, is that our "names are written in heaven" (Luke 10:20). Those that are allowed entrance into glory are "only they that are written in the Lamb's book of life" (Rev. 21:27). So our Hebrews' penman knows the church to have in its fellowship the very people "who are enrolled in heaven." One's name might be found on many lists. There are rolls recording lodge members, class members and club members. The members of the Lord's church have their names written down where it matters — in heaven. There is the real temptation to drop out of the church and avoid the persecution of the world. But, "He that overcometh . . . I (Christ) will in no wise blot his name out of the book of life" (Rev. 3:5).

THE HOLY JUDGE

The eternal heavenly home of the redeemed is the abiding place of "God the Judge of all" (12:23). When men of the world hurl cruel charges at the church, that is no occasion to turn from God's people. It is rather the time to go to God "the Judge of all." At His hand ultimate justice will be dispensed. From Him will come vindication and acquital.

As the Roman epistle exults, "There is . . . now no

condemnation to them that are in Christ Jesus. . . . Who shall lay anything to the charge of God's elect? It is God that justifieth; who is he that condemneth?" (8:1,33-34). Our defense is in God. Run not from Him but to Him and you are secure. He is a "father of the fatherless, and a judge of the widows" (Psa. 68:5). He is "Our Maker, Defender, Redeemer and Friend."[2]

THE HOLY SPIRITS

Not only is "God the Judge of all" in the "heavenly Jerusalem." According to our text, in the city of the living God are "the spirits of just men made perfect" (12:23). Their bodies, as of the writing of the epistle, still await the return of Christ and their resurrection from the grave. Yet, at the moment death separates the spirit from the body that housed it, heaven becomes its home.

This was Paul's certain confidence. He wrote, "For to me to live is Christ, and to die is gain . . . to depart and be with Christ . . . is very far better" (Phil. 1:21-23). He was ever "willing . . . to be absent from the body, and to be at home with the Lord" (II Cor. 5:8). Had not Paul, as he guarded the garments of those stoning Stephen, heard the martyr's triumphant cry, "Lord Jesus, receive my spirit" (Acts 7:59)?

While believers are justified, or acquitted, the day they are cleansed by Christ's blood, these "just men" are "made perfect" later when in God's presence. While in the body, they already had to say, "Not that I have already obtained, or am already made perfect: but I press on" (Phil. 3:12). Now at the end of the Calvary road, by grace, the forgiven in God's presence can be called "the spirits of just men made perfect" (Heb. 12:23).

THE HOLY COVENANT

Since the ascension and until the second coming, Jesus is at the right hand of the Father in heaven. In listing the benefits of choosing Mount Zion over Mount Sinai, or grace over law, we next hear of "Jesus the mediator of a new covenant" (12:24).

In bringing in the new covenant, Christ was creating a new Israel. At the giving of the old covenant to the Israelites at Sinai, God was forming his old theocracy. After the exodus from Egypt, these descendants of Jacob were God's chosen nation. Through them would come the long hoped for Messiah. He would fulfil the prophecies and bring salvation for all men.

Now that the new age has come there can be neither racial limitations nor restrictions of any other kind. Since Pentecost A.D. 30, there "can be neither Jew nor Greek, there can be neither bond nor free, there can be no male and female" (Gal. 3:28). God's new Israel is multi-racial and multi-national. No one is denied citizenship who accepts Jesus as his Saviour and King.

Where many of the promises to the physical descendants of Abraham, Isaac and Jacob were material of nature, those under Jesus' new covenant are primarily of the more spiritual and lasting kind.

This final, holy covenant is entered also in a different way than the earlier contract. Where in the former Sinaitic covenant the physical birth to Jewish parents brought every Israelite into the covenant community; under the "new covenant," the accident of physical birth does not determine one's covenant relationship with God. Personal acceptive response to Christ's offer, is now what matters. To enter the kingdom of God requires a birth of "water and the Spirit. . . . That which is born of the flesh is flesh; and that which is born of the Spirit is spirit" (John 3:5-6).

The old covenant had become "old and . . . aged." It was "nigh unto vanishing away" (Heb. 8:13). The new agreement made both Jews and Gentiles "amen" the apostolic announcement that "ye are all sons of God, through faith in Christ Jesus. For as many of you as were baptized into Christ did put on Christ. . . . And if ye are Christ's, then are ye Abraham's seed, heirs according to promise" (Gal. 3:26-29).

THE HOLY BLOOD

The seventh and final appeal at this point in Hebrews is to stay with "the blood of sprinkling that speaketh better than of Abel (12:24). How is speaking of Christ's blood "better?" The blood of Abel was shed in anger by his brother Cain. Jehovah tells the guilty murderer, "Thy brother's blood crieth unto me from the ground" (Gen. 4:10). The blood of Abel cried for vengeance. The blood of Jesus was freely given a ransom for the many. Christ's blood is a cry to the Holy Father for mercy to be given penitent sinners. Do you not agree Jesus' blood "speaketh better than that of Abel" (12:24)? It calls for mercy rather than vengeance.

CHOOSING MOUNTAINS

The way of works-righteousness always will fall short. Deserved condemnation will come. The way of justification by trust in Christ's proffered righteousness offers forgiveness without fail. Choose life, not death. Opt for mercy, not condemnation. The hymn "Rock of Ages" places before us the same argument as Hebrews: "Not the labors of my hands can fulfill Thy law's demand; Could my zeal no respite know, Could my tears forever flow, all for sin could not atone; Thou must save, and Thou alone."[3]

There is a "sanctification (a holiness) without which no man shall see the Lord" (Heb. 12:14). Be assured, salvation is "not of works that no man should glory" (Eph. 2:9). Let him who has ears to hear and a mind to ponder the opposite outcomes of his choice, ask for mercy not justice. Choose grace first, last and always.

Endnotes

1. "The Ways," in *The Treasury of Religious Verse* (Westwood, NJ: Fleming H. Revell Co., 1962), p. 98.
2. Robert Grant, "O Worship the King," *Favorite Hymns: Number Two* (Cincinnati: Standard Publishing Co., 1941), p. 5.
3. A.M. Toplady, *Favorite Hymns: Number Two* (Cincinnati: Standard Publishing Co., 1942), p. 163.

CHAPTER TWENTY-ONE

Jesus Never Fails
Hebrews 13:1-17

(The Appeal to Love)

"Earthly friends may prove untrue, Doubts and fears assail; One still loves and cares for you: Jesus never fails."[1]

School teachers have had the experience of doing everything possible to assist their students and yet, in spite of every effort finding that not a few will fail. Investors occasionally get leary about their investments, when a news report reaches them that another bank has failed. Specially trained military men can carry out a well-devised plan to release hostages, only to find that the best of human plans has failed again. You may one day find that, after robust years of vigor, health can fail.

The author of the epistle to the Hebrews is not willing to welcome the thought that a Christian would fail Jesus Christ. Most certainly Jesus will not fail his disciple. While the former is possible, the latter could never be. The writer is basing his plea on this fact. The people ought never fail their Lord, because Jesus will never fail them.

In this final chapter of the epistle all the previous reasoning reaches the plea to not turn back from Christianity to Judaism. God spoke to the fathers through human and angelic messengers, but His final message has been delivered to us through His only Son (chapters 1-2). Israel was delivered gloriously by Moses and Joshua. Yet, that rescue fades in significance when compared to the deliverance from sin obtained by Jesus (chapters 2-3). The Old Testament introduces us to the priestly mediation of Melchizedek and the sons of Aaron. That foreshadowing type was followed by the perfect ministry of intercession being performed through Christ our High Priest (chapters 5-7). It naturally followed that the covenant of Sinai, while good, was replaced by a new covenant that is far better (8-10). Should any convert from Judaism to Christianity feel a tug to return to his former religion, he would be going from the greatest hope ever given to man to something less. Chapter 11 called them to hold to their faith. Chapter 12 appealed to the readers to hold courageously to their hope. Chapter 13 is the final call to hold to their love.

The first verse reads, "Let love of the brethren continue." The verses that follow are the development of that plea. There are here what we might call love's ten commandments and its threefold promise. By the time we reach verse 17, we have heard ten imperatives that all who are Christian ought to obey.

TEN LOVE COMMANDMENTS

Thou Shalt Not Fail to Be Brotherly

The first of ten commands could be worded, "Thou

shalt not fail to be brotherly." The word for love in 13:1 is φιλαδελφία. It is not the word ἔρως (selfish, sexual love). It is not the word ἀγάπη (intelligent goodwill). It is rather the word that means brotherly love. The idea is that, if we constitute the family of God, let us act like family. Let us not break away from the family, as some in that early century were tempted to do. Nero was the emperor. A great hostility was being brought against the church. Persecution was directed at the people who were called Christian. The particular believers who were receiving this epistle had been brought to faith in Christ by Paul during his Roman imprisonment. Since, long before, the government had recognized these synagogues as Jewish gatherings, it had escaped them that now they had become Christian-Jewish assemblies. The present fires of persecution would pass them by, should these believers in Jesus as Messiah revert to being simply Jews again. But to do that, they would have to turn their backs on the family of God purchased by the redemption of Christ. Hence the command, "Let love of the brethren continue," or "Thou shalt not fail to be brotherly."

Thou Shalt Not Fail to Be Hospitable

We are next counselled to be hospitable, opening our homes to brethren in need. The persecution was driving fellow-believers out of their homes. As those in flight passed through, they, though unknown by face to their hosts, were to be helped as part of the family.

The command reads, "Forget not to show love unto strangers" (v. 2). The motivation is heightened by the words, "for thereby some have entertained angels unawares." I do not want to destroy your understanding of this verse by my thoughts, but I will share my opinion as to the meaning. When brethren fleeing in their need find refuge in your home, you do not have time to check their name, their address, their occupation, their relatives or whether they are worthy. Those in flight are escaping underground and you have opened your doors to them. You are taking some serious chances. But, do you know, it may be that this brother whom you kept a night or two and then aided on his way, was a preacher of the gospel. He, unaware to you, may have been a "messenger" of the cross.

Angel is but a Greek word meaning messenger. Our word evangelist has the word angel at its heart. The proclaimer of the word is a messenger of the good news. The writer is calling attention to the fact that as one aids another who is a "stranger" to him, it may be that the brother is a Billy Graham or a Dwight L. Moody of that century whom God is using to His glory. The one you may help tomorrow could be a Luther or a Timothy. You knew he was a Christian, but you may not have learned what service he rendered for the Lord. Thou shalt not fail to be hospitable.

Thou Shalt Not Fail to Be Concerned
Each verse so far is a commandment. Verse 1 called for brotherly love, verse 2 for hospitality and verse 3 for concern regarding people imprisoned. Jail was a common experience to early churchmen. It came as no surprise. In his Sermon on the Mount Jesus warned those that would follow him of their coming plight. He said, "Blessed are they that are persecuted for righteousness

sake: for theirs is the kingdom of heaven. Blessed are ye when men shall reproach you, and persecute you, and say all manner of evil against you falsely, for my sake" (Matt. 5:10-11).

Peter remembered Jesus' words and passed similar counsel on to his readers. Approximately four years before the epistle of Hebrews, Peter had written these words:

> Beloved, think it not strange concerning the fiery trial among you, which cometh upon you to prove you, as though a strange thing happened unto you . . . but if a man suffer as a Christian, let him not be ashamed; but let him glorify God in this name (I Pet. 4:12,16).

At the final judgment there will be people surprised at the King's words, "Inherit the kingdom . . . for I was in prison, and ye came unto me" (Matt. 25:34,36). Are you surprised to learn that Jesus anticipated that Christian history, from first to last, would record his "brethren" being "in prison" and in need of visitation?

This makes appropriate the plea, "Remember them that are in bonds, as bound with them; them that are ill-treated, as being yourselves also in the body" (Heb. 13:3). Neither fail Christ in brotherliness, hospitality nor concern.

Thou Shalt Not Fail to Be Chaste

The next two commands call for chastity (v. 4) and honesty (v. 5). They read, "Let marriage be had in honor among all, and let the bed be undefiled: for fornicators and adulterers God will judge. Be ye free from the love of money; content with such things as ye have: for himself hath said, I will in no wise fail thee."

When a selfless servant of the Lord opens his or her abode to a person in want, respect for the ethical standards of that Lord requires righteousness. Shall a Priscilla and Aquila be rewarded for their love of brothers by a violation of their possessions? Shall a Mary or her son Mark find the lust to the flesh overpowering their new night-guest to the defilement of the marriage bed?

Even in the church the warning needs to be heard at any moment of potential weakness: "Let the marriage be had in honor among all, and let the bed be undefiled: for fornicators and adulterers God will judge" (13:4).

Thou Shalt Not Fail to Be Honest

Imagine a Christian running for his life. A fellow believer allows him into his house for the night. What the next day might hold is unknown to him. Might Satan fill his heart to pilfer some valuable in the host's abode that could give him the means needed for another day of life? Let him remember that the house he is in and all its possessions belong to another. He must be honest. He is a follower of Christ. Let him recall that God will provide for his needs. Let him be "free from the love of money" and remain "content with such things" as he has. Let him remember the Father's promise, "I will in no wise fail thee, neither will I in any wise forsake thee. So that with good courage we say, 'The Lord is my helper; I will not fear: What shall man do unto me?'" (13:5-6).

Each Christian is a human. Temptations come to believer and unbeliever alike. It is vital to remember who we have promised to serve and to whom we have vowed our loyalty. In the situation where large numbers of the church are fleeing for their lives and seeking refuge in the middle of the night, there is need that each one retain not only his faith and hope but his brotherly love. Even Jesus' followers need admonition to remember their commitment to the way of Christ. The way of holiness is a way of purity and honesty. Let no shame be brought upon the church by touching another man's wife or another man's belongings. The Head of the church will provide his people's needs. They will not need to grasp the possessions of another.

Thou Shalt Not Fail to Be Grateful

One powerful motivation to godly living is the example of those that brought us to the faith and have nurtured us in the gospel. Therefore the next appeal is: "Remember them that had the rule over you, men that spake unto you the word of God; and considering the issue of their life, imitate their faith" (13:7).

What a spur to righteousness is the happy remembrance of the messengers that brought to us the good tidings! What a lift toward Christ-likeness is the recalling of the individuals who led us to Jesus in the first place! The very thought of them brings a gratitude that holds us true.

Remember the ones who brought you to the faith. Call to mind Peter and Paul. See again in your heart the faces of your fathers in the gospel. They remained true to the end. Can we fail them? Dare we fail Him? Gratitude demands loyalty.

Thou Shalt Not Fail to Be Consistent

Some people are unreliable. One day you could count on them, but not the next day. One time they believed one way, now they have changed their doctrine. How comforting to learn that "Jesus Christ is the same yesterday and today, yea and forever" (13:8). How disheartening it is to know that some believers are about to change back from the New Covenant to the Old.

The writer begs, "Be not carried away by diverse and strange teachings: for it is good that the heart be established by grace; not by meats, wherein they that occupied themselves were not profited" (13:9). Grace is where our feet should be planted. The physical things of the tabernacle and the period of the law pointed to the lasting spiritual things of the eternal gospel. Once having turned to the higher and the better way of Christ, let not even one go back to lower ground.

The admonition is to remain true to the apostolic teaching that marked the church from its beginning. That faith was "once for all delivered unto the saints" (Jude 3). Paul, Peter, John and the other apostles revealed the mind of Christ to their generation. To be lured away to some new thing because of itching ears, is to start on a dead-end road that does not lead to life. To be "carried away by diverse . . . teachings" is to leave the one way of salvation for the many ways that lead to nowhere.

Thou Shalt Not Fail to Be Separate

Verses 10 and 11 remind the reader how that in olden days the ministers in the tabernacle burned the offering for sin "without the camp." Verse 12 points to Jesus who, to "sanctify the people through his own blood, suffered without the gate." This leads to the logical appeal of verse 13 that the readers must "go forth unto him without the camp."

This is a clear call for a break with Judaism. If the scriptural type was burned "without the camp" and Jesus died "without the gate," loyalty to the Lord now called on the Jewish Christians to go outside the protection of their synagogue and show alignment with the suffering believers in Jesus. That may be the decision now demanded by their covenant with the Savior. Leaving Judaism would expose them to persecution. But faithfulness to Jesus at this hour may demand it. Hear the call, "Go forth unto him without the camp." There will be ridicule. There may be shame. But cut the tie that holds to the past, though it carry with it "bearing his reproach."

Thou Shalt Not Fail to Be Evangelistic

In the priesthood of all belivers, where every man is a priest, what sacrifice have we to offer? Since Christ's perfect sacrifice for sin leaves none other to be offered, what are we to offer as mediators between God and man?

The answer is, "Let us offer up a sacrifice of praise to God continually." Should we further inquire what that may be, the author continues, "that is, the fruit of the lips which make confession to his name" (13:15). Every convert Paul made he counted his sacrifice to God. He wrote of "the offering up of the Gentiles" (Rom. 15:16). You and I can "do good and . . . communicate . . . for with such sacrifices God is well pleased" (Heb. 13:16).

Thou Shalt Not Fail to Be Obedient

The tenth command of Hebrews 13 is the imperative:

"Obey them that have the rule over you, and submit to them: for they watch in behalf of your souls, as they that shall give account; that they may do this with joy, and not with grief: for this were unprofitable for you" (v. 17).

The passage makes clear that, while some members were considering a break from Christianity, no leaders were leaving. The shepherds of the flock were calling for each member of their fold to remain with Christ. Such loyal leaders were to be obeyed. Their rule was not to be challenged but submitted to.

The Three-fold Promise
It matters not that we know who wrote this letter. It might have been Paul, Apollos, or some other. What is of supreme import is that we glean the ten admonitions that will keep a Christian faithful to his Christ. As the reader hears the ten commands, he also hears three encouraging promises. These promises stir the heart to remain faithful to Jesus Christ.

Yesterday
Be reminded that "Jesus Christ is the same yesterday, and today, yea and forever" (13:8). You realize then that he will not fail you. The "yesterday" of this verse is not the eternal yesterday but the historic yesterday of the Lord's incarnation. The events recorded in the Gospel reveal the life and teachings of Jesus in the flesh. Do the Synoptics or John ever tell of Christ failing someone?

The reading of these New Testament books reminds us of people who failed him. There was Judas who betrayed him. There was Peter that denied him. There was a Jewish nation that would not receive him as the Messiah. There were religious leaders among Pharisees and Sadducees that he found it necessary to label hypocrites. Yes, others failed Jesus; but, in that yesterday of his incarnate life, did he ever fail anyone?

Did he ever fail a child? When others tried to keep the small ones from him, he lifted them to his lap and said, "Suffer the little children, and forbid them not, to come unto me: for to such belongeth the kingdom of heaven" (Matt. 19:13-14).

Did the Lord ever fail a woman? Note his ministry to the woman whom he found at the Samaritan well. Whatever the need or wherever the place, the Master ministered with concern. This Son of God never failed a sick person. He never failed a leper. Healing and cleansing was in his touch.

Did the Saviour ever fail a sinner? Did he not rather speak encouragement to those caught in the very act of iniquity, "Neither do I condemn thee: go thy way; from henceforth sin no more" (John 8:11). A review of Biblical material makes evident that, while in the yesterdays people failed Jesus, Jesus never failed people. Even despised tax-collectors were told, "Today I must abide at thy house" (Luke 19:5).

Today

While that was true concerning Jesus yesterday, what is true today? Has he ever failed me? Has he ever failed you? He promised, "Ask, and it shall be given you" (Matt. 7:7). He instructed, "Hitherto have ye asked nothing in my name: ask, and ye shall receive, that your joy may be made full" (John 16:24). Has he ever failed you, when you prayed?

Do you feel lonesome today? Remember he assured, "Lo, I am with you always even unto the end" (Matt. 28:20). Has he failed there? Have you gone to a graveside, wondering if Jesus really cared? A moment of reflection brings the certainty that while we may fail him, he is always there. He never forsakes his people. He never turns his back on their need. He is always at our side when we need him most.

Forever

What was true yesterday and today will remain true through all the tomorrows. "Jesus Christ is the same yesterday and today, yea and forever" (Heb. 13:8). His promise is "I will in no wise fail thee, neither will I in any wise forsake thee. So that with good courage we say, The Lord is my helper; I will not fear: What shall man do unto me?" (13:5-6).

The covenant God has made with you and me may be broken. But it will never be broken from the Divine side. If it is broken, it will be broken from the human side. The plea of Hebrews is that if he will never fail us, how can we contemplate ever failing him? Of all trusted friends, best of all is Jesus.

Endnotes

1. Arthur A. Luther, "Jesus Never Fails" *Favorite Hymns of Praise* (Wheaton, IL: Tabernacle Pub. Co., 1967). p. 165. Copyright Singspiration, Inc.

CHAPTER TWENTY-TWO

Eyes on the Future
Hebrews 13:14-21

(The Appeal to Submission)

To oversee the flock of God is a great responsibility. To overlook His sheep is a perilous failure. The persons especially assigned to care for the fold of Christ are sometimes called overseers (bishops), sometimes elders, sometimes shepherds (pastors) and sometimes rulers.

The final chapter of Hebrews issues this call to the church: Obey them that have the rule over you, and submit to them: for they watch in behalf of your souls, as they that shall give account" (13:17). The word "ruler" is a common Bible term often applied to those men who served either local Jewish synagogues or Christian assemblies. The Jews spoke of such functionaries as the rulers or the elders of their synagogue. Their mission was to guide the people according to the Scriptures. This terminology of the synagogue passed over into that of the church.

Note now the change in verb tense from verse 7 to

verse 17 of our chapter. The former reads, "Remember them that had the rule over you." The latter calls for submission to "them that have the rule over you." Those that "had" the rule in earlier days possibly were men like Peter or Paul or James. Peter was martyred in A.D. 64 and James in A.D. 66. Paul had been beheaded in 67. It is now about A.D. 68 as the epistle is written. These former leaders are gone. They are to be remembered with respect. The present rulers are to be obeyed with appreciation. The benediction that follows, points beyond the rulers on earth to the Ruler of heaven. This Ruler of rulers, this Pastor of pastors is Jesus "the great shepherd of the sheep" (13:20). We find the chapter has moved from past overseers, to present overseers and finally to the eternal overseer, or shepherd, Christ.

If overseers are to watch over the church, let us learn which direction their eyes should be looking. It is through the vision of our under-shepherds that we should get a glimpse of God's will for us.

LOOK TO THE FUTURE

The danger facing the original readers of our epistle was looking back. Their eyes were turning from Christ to the Old Covenant, the ancient temple and its holy city of Jerusalem. They are jolted to remember that "we have not here an abiding city, but we seek after the city which is to come" (13:14).

Consider the historic situation. Jerusalem and its temple were not going to last. In a short time it would collapse as Jesus had predicted, leaving not "one stone upon another" (Matt. 24:2). You know that this destructive event occurred in A.D. 70. Any man that turned back to the temple, its priesthood and its rituals was left with nothing.

Those in Jerusalem who had believed Jesus and followed his counsel, escaped Judaea unharmed. They recalled Christ's teaching, "But when ye see Jerusalem compassed with armies, then know that her desolation is at hand. Then let them that are in Judaea flee unto the mountains" (Luke 21:20-21). According to Josephus 1,700,000 were killed. The Christians of the land escaped to Pella unharmed, for they followed the forewarning of Christ.

The Hebrews' writer, about two years prior to Jerusalem's desolation, shouts out, "We have not here an abiding city." He points rather to the heavenly Jerusalem, "the city which is to come." A believer should make his goal neither the past nor the present. His eyes should look to the future. Let him be "forgetting the things which are behind, and stretching forward to the things which are before" (Phil. 3:13).

Racers win who do not look to the right or the left but toward the goal. As earlier admonished by the "great cloud of witnesses" from the past and the epistle's author in the present, all eyes should be "looking unto Jesus" (12:1-2). Myopia or near-sightedness must be avoided by all church overseers. Long range vision is needed. Should those living for eternity only lay plans for thirty days and leave unexplored where a congregation should be in a decade? While the eternal future should be in the consciousness of elders planning a congregation's strategy, that only should make them better prepared to hammer out wise plans for the work yet to be accomplished on earth. Looking to the future should become a guiding principle to those trusted with oversight.

LOOK TO THE FATHER

With the eyes wide open we look forward to the future with hope. With clear vision we look up to the Father with praise, for adoration ever is fitting. "Through him (Christ) then let us offer up a sacrifice of praise to God continually, that is, the fruit of lips which make confession to his name" (13:15). To the church the direction is onward and upward ever.

What is the value of constant gratitude and praise? The redeemed are those that are grateful. The lost are the ungrateful. The epistle to the Romans describes the devolution of man. It says that "knowing God, they glorified him not as God, neither gave thanks" (v. 21). While created by God and blessed by Him, men neglected to look up in gratitude to the One above them. They thus began to live like the animals beneath them.

The unpardonable sin, the sin against the Holy Spirit, can be explained in various ways, but the bottom line of that sin without pardon is ingratitude. After all the centuries of preparation and planning by God to bring the Savior into the world, some ever will refuse it. Ungrateful men resist and reject every effort of the loving God who longs to save them. Men may call light darkness. They may shut their eyes to Jesus' love and power. But he can give pardon only to those willing to

receive it. Ingratitude leaves only perdition.
Christian men live by the Scriptures:

> Let the word of Christ dwell in you richly; in all wisdom teaching and admonishing one another with psalms and hymns and spiritual songs, singing with grace in your hearts unto God. And whatsoever ye do, in word or in deed, do all in the name of the Lord Jesus, giving thanks to God the Father through him (Col. 3:16-17).

The reason you assemble with the saints on the Lord's Day is that you appreciate what God has done for the world. Why have you responded to the gospel invitation to belong to Christ? Because you thankfully received the offered forgiveness. The trait of the saved is appreciation. The mark of the lost is the opposite. It is ingratitude.

LOOK TO THE FLOCK

A sergeant may command, "Eyes right!" Hebrews 13 commands, "Eyes forward! Eyes upward! Eyes outward!" After the encouragement to look on to the future and up to the Father, comes the urging to look out to the flock: "But to do good and to communicate forget not: for with such sacrifices God is well pleased" (13:16).

God's people do have needs. We are to look to the meeting of those needs. As James said, "Pure religion and undefiled before our God and Father is this, to visit the fatherless and widows in their affliction, and to keep oneself unspotted from the world" (James 1:27).

Tithing at the weekly assembly is not a substitute for

helping the needy soul that comes your way the next day. Jesus spoke to his disciples regarding almsgiving. The Bible calls for believers to show care to all people in want, "especially toward them that are of the household of the faith" (Gal. 6:10).

The "sacrifices" with which "God is well pleased" are said to be doing good and communicating. What is doing good? That is helpful service. What is communication or fellowship? That, too, is sharing. This reminds us all that believers are not to be so heavenly minded that they are of no earthly use. Rather, they are to "do good" and fellowship or "communicate" with the family. The eyes of God are upon them. Their eyes must ever be upon God's family. While the Christians can offer no blood sacrifice for the sins of the people, they can offer beneficial service for the needs of those people. "With such sacrifices God is well pleased" (13:16).

Hebrews 10:25 spoke of some converts who were "forsaking . . . assembling together." That became a primary responsibility of the overseers and their helpers the deacons. The Good Shepherd had taught his followers well that a fold of one hundred sheep was not to be considered secure when only ninety-nine were accounted for. Going out to recover the missing sheep costs effort and requires time. But it is "with such sacrifices God is well pleased." No elder dare forget the flock over which he is given oversight. Each must pay the price to be counted a faithful pastor for the Lord.

LOOK TO THE FAITH

"Obey . . . submit . . . for they watch in behalf of

your souls" (13:17). I sense an underlying concern for doctrine here. Elders "shall give account" for the souls entrusted to their care. With some, the responsibility is a "joy." With others, it is a "grief."

Be reminded what a "ruler" is in Biblical terminology. Rulers in the church are not dictators nor business executives. We call yard-sticks, "rulers" by which one can measure. The Carpenter of Nazareth gave revelation by which our faith and practices should be measured. The elders, or rulers, are to be obeyed. The members under their care are to submit to their application of the measuring rod of Christ. The shepherds ought to know pure water from poisoned water better than this ewe or that lamb.

Please be aware of the clear distinction between making rules and applying rules. Church elders were given from heaven no authority for making rules. Their job is not to legislate but to apply. They do not make the standards. They see that in their arena of authority, those norms set down by Christ's apostles are complied with. No overseer is to order obedience to a human opinion. He is to "measure the temple of God . . . and them that worship" (Rev. 11:1) by the divinely furnished standard.

Paul found some in the church to be "children tossed to and fro and carried about with every wind of doctrine" (Eph. 4:14). You have discovered others susceptible to cult teaching that pulls them this way or to denominational dogma that tugs them another way. How happy is the shepherd who finds his people led by the apostles' teaching.

Some foolishly say that doctrine doesn't matter, but that only love does. Yet every epistle in the New Testament is written to call the recipients to follow the apostles' doctrine. The epistles of John warn of the antichrists in the world. Whereas "the liar . . . denieth that Jesus is the Christ" (I John 2:22), the true prophet "confesseth that Jesus Christ is come in the flesh" (4:2). That is a doctrinal concern.

Most every Bible book written from Ephesus, or to someone in Ephesus, warns of the heresy later called gnosticism. Several of Paul's letters call on the readers to beware the Judaizers. All of the sacred writings oppose any doctrine that veers from the teaching of Christ preserved by his apostles. God placed in every congregation shepherds to see that the flock drink in good waters unpoisoned by error. The overseers' task includes watching to see that the truth of Christ is not adulterated with the traditions of men. "The faith which was once for all delivered unto the saints" (Jude 3) is to remain the message of the church in every century until Christ returns.

LOOK TO THE FORCE

Three little words introduce the final appeal (Heb. 13:18-19) that will lead to the benediction (13:20-21) and concluding instructions (13:22-25). The three little words "Pray for us," suggest the source of the church's power to carry out its mission. The greatest force in the world is prayer.

Prayer changes things. Prayer changes people. Prayer changes even those who do the praying. Prayer is the force that transforms everything.

Whoever wrote Hebrews held the same high view of intercession as did the apostle John who said, "We have boldness toward God; and whatsoever we ask we receive of him" (I John 3: 21-22). Whoever penned our epistle of study had the conviction that moved Paul to write, "pray without ceasing" (I Thess. 5:17). Whoever gave us this marvelous book on the superiority of Christ, shared the attitude of the Master himself. Jesus ever uged his disciples to "ask . . . seek . . . and . . . knock" (Matt. 7:7) at heaven's door. Whoever was used of the Holy Spirit as amanuensis for this work knew prayer as the force enabling every good work and as the source providing every needed ability.

Prayer is the power of God. And God "is able to do exceeding abundantly above all that we ask or think, according to the power that worketh in us" (Eph. 3:20). While no one questions that "the gospel . . . is the power of God unto salvation" (Rom. 1:16), and that this message works powerfully in us, we also know prayer to be an enabling force for workers who preach that gospel. No sooner has Paul described for the Ephesians "the sword of the Spirit" as "the word of God," than he points to "prayer and supplication" (Eph. 6:17-18). He who has all the armor of God is well protected defensively from Satan's onslaught. But, he who will accomplish aggressively the conquest of the Devil's domain, for Christ, will only win such evangelistic triumphs by the power of prayer. That will require "all prayer and supplication . . . at all seasons in the Spirit."

The book of Hebrews, like its final chapter, is a call to every believer to be a hopeful, grateful, concerned, reliable and prayerful person. It is a plea for every congregation to be marked by vision, appreciation, brotherly love, faithfulness, and contact with God. As "His eye is on the sparrow," may our eyes see clearly each opportunity to minister for Him as it is brought our way.

CONCLUSION

Choose the Best

Men are free to agree or disagree with the assertion of Hebrews that "better" is the term that uniquely fits the Christian faith. In thorough and extended examination of the claims made by religious leaders across the centuries, I am compelled to conclude that best of all is Jesus.

If Jesus is the Christ and God's only begotten Son, then there is hope for our world. Love, kindness, and tender concern is deified rather than cruelty and hate being crowned. Bring to mind every virtue you can imagine. Jesus is that good personified.

Is God, the world's Creator and Sustainer, like Jesus? Does He care for children and widows in need, as the Master Teacher from Galilee taught? Is He touched by the hurts and concerns of all races, all classes and all kinds? Do love and power balance in His dealings with men, as they did in the ministry of the Carpenter of

BEST OF ALL IS JESUS

Nazareth? Would a God exactly like Jesus be too good to be true? For two thousand years the only logical conclusion that multitudes have been able to draw, is that Jesus is Lord and the Christian faith is too good not to be true. Reject all that is evil. Refuse all that is unworthy. Gather together only what purports to be good. Evaluate and rate these by comparison, isolating the "better." Filtering every valuable person, place or thing in history through the sieve of love and truth, there remains but one worthy of worship. Of all who claim our full allegiance, best of all is Jesus. Car dealers may say, "If you can find a better car, buy it." Salesmen may argue, "If you can get a better deal, take it." I know you will never hear of a better Saviour. Take Christ into your life, for best of all is Jesus!

APPENDIX

One Preacher's Analysis of Another Preacher's Sermon

I. *GOD'S MESSENGER IS WORTHY OF OUR LOYALTY* (Heb. 1:1-2:18)
   A. Consider Seven Facts about Jesus (1:1-3).
      1. Heir
      2. Creator
      3. Glorious
      4. Image
      5. Sustainer
      6. Saviour
      7. King
   B. Consider Seven Texts from the Bible (1:4-14).
      1. Psa. 2:7 calls Jesus "son."
      2. II Sam. 7:14 calls Jesus "son."
      3. Psa. 97:7 says "worship him."
      4. Psa. 104:4 calls angels "ministers."
      5. Psa. 45:6-7 calls Jesus "God."
      6. Psa. 102:25-27 calls Jesus "Lord."
      7. Psa. 110:1 invites Jesus to sit at God's "right hand."
   C. Consider Getting Justice, If We Reject Him (2:5-18).
   D. Consider Getting Help, If We Call on Him (2:5-18).
      1. The future is meant for you (2:5-8).
      2. The past required suffering from Jesus (2:9-10).
      3. The present requires suffering from you (2:11-15).
      4. The present offers help to you (2:16-18).

II. *GOD'S DELIVERER IS WORTHY OF OUR LOYALTY* (3:1-4:16)
   A. Consider Jesus' Superiority to Moses (3:1-6).

B. Consider Israel's Failure to Remain Faithful (3:7-19).
 1. The way it was for most of Israel (7-11).
 2. The way it was not to be for any of the church (12-14).
 3. The sin to be avoided (15-19).
    a. The refusal to listen (15-16).
    b. The refusal to obey (17-18).
    c. The refusal to trust (19).
C. Consider the Church's Need to Remain Faithful (4:1-16).
 1. Through Moses came a day of rest (1-6).
 2. Through Joshua came a land of rest (7-8).
 3. Through Jesus came the heavenly rest (9-11).
 4. God's word can be a sword of judgment (12-13).
 5. God's Son can be a shield of protection (14-16).

III. *GOD'S MEDIATOR IS WORTHY OF OUR LOYALTY* (5:1-7:28).
 A. Consider Jesus' Superiority to Aaronic Priests (5:1-10).
  1. He is from God rather than men (1).
  2. He offers himself rather than animals (2).
  3. He is sinless rather than sinful (2-3).
  4. He is God's Son rather than God's servant (4-5).
  5. He is eternal rather than temporal (6).
  6. He is perfect rather than inadequate (7-10).
 B. Consider the Recipients' Condition (5:11-6:20).
  1. Their immaturity (5:11-14).
  2. Their need to grow (6:1-3).
  3. Their possible danger (6:4-8).
  4. Their encouraging signs (6:9-12).
  5. Their example in Abraham (6:13-15).

6. Their hope in Jesus (6:16-20).
C. Consider Jesus' Likeness to Melchizedek (7:1-10).
   1. Jesus is a priest-king (1-2).
   2. Jesus is a king of righteousness.
   3. Jesus is a king of peace.
   4. Jesus is unique.
   5. Jesus is a receiver of tithes (4-10).
   6. Jesus is a giver of blessings.
D. Consider Jesus' Dissimilarity to Levites (7:11-28).
   1. Jesus is under a different law (11-12).
   2. Jesus is from a different tribe (13-14).
   3. Jesus ministers for a different period of time (15-17).
   4. Jesus obtains a different result (18-25).
   5. Jesus is of a different character (26-28).

IV. *GOD'S COVENANT IS WORTHY OF OUR LOYALTY* (8:1-10:39).
   A. Consider the Better Covenant (8:1-13).
      1. It has a new capital (1).
      2. It has a new tabernacle (2-5).
      3. It has new terms (6-9).
      4. It has new parties (10-11).
      5. It has new promises (12-13).
   B. Consider the Better Tabernacle (9:1-28).
      1. The old tabernacle had certain furniture (1-5).
      2. The old tabernacle had a temporal ministry (6-10).
      3. The new tabernacle has an eternal ministry (11-28).
         a. Essential to our redemption is Christ's blood (11-14).
         b. Essential to our inheritance is Christ's death (15-22).

  c. Essential to his intercession is Christ's ascension (23-26).
  d. Essential to our salvation is Christ's return (27-28).
 C. Consider the Better Sacrifice (10:1-39).
  1. An appeal to the reader's reason (1-18).
  2. An appeal to the reader's loyalty (19-25).
  3. An appeal to the reader's fear (26-31).
  4. An appeal to the reader's memory (32-39).

V. *GOD'S CALL FOR LOYALTY TO HIS SON* (11:1-13:19).
 A. Hear the Appeal for Abiding Faith (11:1-40).
  1. Our faith should be like that of the patriarchs (1-7).
  2. Our faith should be like that of Abraham, Isaac, and Jacob (8-22).
  3. Our faith should be like that of Moses and Joshua (23-31).
  4. Our faith should be like the Old Testament heroes (32-40).
 B. Hear the Appeal for Abiding Hope (12:1-29).
  1. Learn a lesson from runners (1-3).
  2. Learn a lesson from fathers (4-13).
  3. Learn a lesson from Esau (14-17).
  4. Learn a lesson from Sinai (18-29).
 C. Hear the Appeal for Abiding love (13:1-19).
  1. Love is hospitable (1-2).
  2. Love is supportive (3).
  3. Love is pure (4).
  4. Love is honest (5-6).
  5. Love is apostolic (7-9).
  6. Love is self-sacrificing (10-14).
  7. Love is grateful (15-16).
  8. Love is submissive (17).
  9. Love is prayerful (18-19).

APPENDIX

CONCLUSION
    A. The Benediction (20-21).
    B. The Appeal (22-24).
    C. The Salvation (25).